An EU Charter of Fundamental Rights

ʁs by the last date below.
ɑrged on overdue books
ɑte of 5p per day.

Text and commentaries

edited by

Kim Feus

constitution for europe
FEDERAL TRUST SERIES 1

The Federal Trust

The Federal Trust's aim is to enlighten public debate on federal issues of national, continental and global government. It does this in the light of its statutes which state that it shall promote 'studies in the principles of international relations, international justice and supranational government.'

The Trust conducts enquiries, promotes seminars and conferences and publishes reports, books and teaching materials.

The Trust is the UK member of the Trans-European Policy Studies Association (TEPSA), a grouping of fifteen think tanks from Member States of the European Union.

This book is the first in the Federal Trust's 'Constitution for Europe' series. Further volumes will include *A Simplified Treaty. Text and commentaries* and *The Treaty of Nice. Analysis and commentaries*.

Up-to-date information about the Federal Trust can be found on the internet at www.fedtrust.co.uk

© Federal Trust for Education and Research 2000

ISBN 1 903403 04 9

The Federal Trust is a Registered Charity No. 272241
Dean Bradley House, 52 Horseferry Road,
London SW1P 2 AF
Company Limited by Guarantee No. 1269848

Printed in the European Union

Contents

Part II Legal Issues

Part III The Content of the EU Charter

Part IV The Charter and Beyond

Editor's note:

Contributors have written their commentaries on the basis of the draft Charter as it stood in July 2000 (CHARTE 4422/00, CONVENT 45). In view of the changes in the final version of September 2000 (CHARTE 4487/00, CONVENT 50) some authors have added postscripts to their contributions. Where reference has been made to specific provisions of the draft, the article numbers have been adjusted to reflect the Charter as approved at the Biarritz Summit in Ocotber 2000.

Contributors

Giampiero Alhadeff is Secretary-General of Solidar, an independent European alliance of NGOs involved in social welfare, life-long learning, development and humanitarian aid. He is also President of the Platform of European Social NGOs, an alliance of thirty NGO networks working in the social field.

Frédérique Bosvieux is Senior Policy Adviser in the Human Resources Directorate of the Confederation of British Industry (CBI), working on employment and labour market issues - in particular, working time and working families' tax credits, European social policy and the EU Charter.

Clare Coffey is Research Fellow at the London based Institute for European Environmental Policy (IEEP). She has a legal background and her key areas of work are EC and international environmental law and policy, such as institutional and strategic issues, and all aspects of EC fisheries policy.

Jonathan Cooper is Director of the Human Rights Project at JUSTICE and Associate Tenant of Doughty Street Chambers. He has taken several cases to the ECtHR and has written and lectured extensively on the Human Rights Act. He is book review editor for the Human Rights Law Review.

Andrew Duff is the Liberal Democrat MEP for Eastern England and Constitutional Affairs Spokesman of the European Liberal Democrats (ELDR). A member of the Convention, he is also the EP's co-rapporteur on the Charter. He was formerly Director of the Federal Trust.

Professor Piet Eeckhout is Herbert Smith Professor of European Law and Director of the Centre of European Law at King's College London. He also teaches at the College of Europe in Bruges and has previously worked in the Chambers of Advocate General Jacobs at the European Court of Justice.

David Feikert is Brussels Officer of the Trades Union Congress (TUC). He has been involved in a wide range of economic and social policy issues. He has presented the TUC in the EU Social Dialogue Committee and acted as an expert for the ETUC on study groups of the Economic and Social Committee.

Dr John Godfrey is a Trustee of European Research into Consumer Affairs (ERICA) and Vice-Chairman of the Consumers in Europe Group. He is also a spokesperson for Action Programme for the Citizens of Europe.

Lord Goldsmith QC is the personal representative of the UK government on the Convention. He is a commercial barrister practising from Fountain Court Chambers and is currently Chairman of the Bar Pro Unit and of the Human Rights Institute of the International Bar Association.

Dr Jackie Gower is Honorary Senior Lecturer in European Politics at the University of Kent at Canterbury. She was the specialist adviser to the recent House of Lords Select Committee *Report on Enlargement of the EU* and has worked on several EU projects in Central and Eastern Europe.

Win Griffiths is the Labour MP for Bridgend and a UK parliamentary member of the Convention. From 1997-98, he has served as Parliamentary Under Secretary of State for Wales. Prior to this, he represented the South Wales constituency in the European Parliament of which he was also Vice President.

Sukhvinder Kaur Stubbs is the Chair of Diversity Works, a new agency promoting diversity in the workplace, and Chair of the European Network Against Racism. A Trustee of DEMOS, MERGE and the UK Asian Womens' Forum, she was formerly also Chief Executive of the Runnymede Trust.

Timothy Kirkhope is Conservative MEP for Yorkshire & The Humber and a member of the Convention. He is also the Conservative spokesman on Justice and Home Affairs and Chief Whip of the British Conservative delegation. From 1987-1997, he served as MP for Leeds North East.

Lord Lester of Herne Hill QC is a practising member of Blackstone Chambers, a Liberal Democrat Peer and an Honorary Visiting Professor at University College London. He specialises in Public law and European Human Rights law and has introduced two Private Members Bills in the Lords to incorporate the ECHR into UK law.

Michael Meehan is lecturer in UK and European Public law at Liverpool John Moores University. He is also researching a PhD on the EU Charter and the constitutionalisation of the EU polity at Birbeck College London. He has previously taught UK Public law at the University of Bordeaux.

Lord Russell-Johnston is President of the Council of Europe Parliamentary Assembly. He has been a Scottish Liberal Democrat Member for Inverness since 1984 and was Leader of the Liberal, Democrat and Reformers' Group and Chairman of the Committee on Culture and Education.

Rósín Pillay is a barrister and the Human Rights Legal Officer at JUSTICE. She focuses on the ECHR and the implementation of the Human Rights Act. She formerly worked at the Irish Law Reform Commission and has written on a variety of law reform and international human rights issues.

Jeremy Smith is Director of the Local Government International Bureau. He is a barrister and has worked in private practice, as legal adviser to the Brent Community Law Centre and as senior policy lawyer with the GLC. He previously was Chief Executive of the London Borough of Camden.

Suzanne Sumner is the Social Affairs Campaigns Officer at SOLIDAR, an alliance of NGOs linked to the trade unions and socialist parties. She is a graduate of the MA in Human Rights at the University of Essex and has been following the drafting process of the Charter of Fundamental Rights in Brussels.

Tony Venables is Director of the Euro Citizen Action Service (ECAS) in Brussels, and a member of the high level panel on free movement of people. Before setting up ECAS, he was Director of the European Bureau of Consumer Unions (BEUC) and worked for the Council of Europe and the Council of Ministers.

Preface

President Chirac, announcing the unanimous agreement of the fifteen Heads of State and Government on the text of the Charter of Fundamental Rights at the Biarritz European Council in October, described it as 'a text which states for the first time the values, principles and essential rights which the peoples of the Union recognise as theirs and which the Union proposes to others to accept if they wish to join us. It is also an ambitious political text which enshrines or confirms principles which often go beyond those already enunciated, for example in the European Convention on Human Rights. I am thinking in particular of social rights and of so-called new rights such as bio-ethical, environmental or data protection rights.'

This is a fundamental text which, once the other institutions of the European Union have approved it, will be proclaimed by the European Council at Nice at the end of the year. The Federal Trust, generously supported by the Joseph Rowntree Charitable Trust, has sponsored a series of seminars at which eminent lawyers, academics, politicians, business and non-government organisations closely involved with human rights and legal issues have presented their views on the Charter as it has developed from one draft to another through the negotiating process. These seminars and this resulting publication are a contribution to the discussion of human rights within the European family of nations, helping to enlighten the debate on a subject often marked by mutual misunderstanding among the participants who approach the subject with markedly different assumptions.

Here the issues are clearly laid out, first in an overview by Lord Lester of Herne Hill, and then in a series of short commentaries by lawyers, politicians, human rights activists, academics, civil servants, trade unions, business and local government representatives. Each contribution is preceded by a

1

short executive summary (in *italics*). After the institutional and political points of view (Part I) come those of the lawyers (Part II), then various views on economic and social rights (Part III) and finally issues of social discrimination, minorities and the impact of the Charter on the process of enlargement for the EU and a citizen's Europe (Part IV). The Charter as approved at Biarritz forms part of the book so that attentive readers can relate the interpretations of the commentators to the text itself.

If the book serves to widen and to enlighten debate on this complex and controversial, yet highly important subject, the Federal Trust will be well pleased.

Martyn Bond
Director

October 2000

Introduction

Lord Lester of Herne Hill

This book makes a timely and stimulating contribution to the debate surrounding the EU Charter. It shows that while there is wide agreement about the need for an EU Charter of Fundamental Rights, there is disagreement over the purpose, status and contents of the Charter. Some contributors see the Charter as a vehicle for the recognition of new rights. Others see it as a way of making socio-economic rights legally enforceable, or of plugging gaps in the protection of civil and political rights, with others viewing it merely as a useful political and rhetorical tool for informing European citizens of their rights. These differences of opinion have been expressed in recent months in the controversy across the EU. In the heat of this controversy, the very real arguments that make some form of Charter necessary have been lost. There is a need for clear and rational analysis of what the Charter is intended to accomplish.

The protection of human rights is part of the political heritage of Member States of the EU. Every European state (within the EU and in the wider Council of Europe) has ratified the European Convention on Human Rights, and has incorporated (or in Ireland's case, is about to incorporate) the Convention into national law. The human rights tradition has not always been visible in the development of the EU. The Community Treaties in their original form contained no requirement for Member States or EU institutions to respect human rights (except in relation to nationality and sex discrimination). Gradually, human rights principles have been woven into EU policies and legal rules. The European Court of Justice has adopted them as 'general principles' of EC law. Article 6 of the Amsterdam Treaty now declares that the Union is 'founded on the principles of liberty, democracy, respect for human rights and fundamental freedoms, and the rule of law', and the requirement to respect fundamental rights is justiciable under Article 46(d) of the Treaty.

In the absence of accession of the Union to the ECHR (which would require a revision of the Treaties), the EU institutions are not directly bound by any international human rights treaties. Nor does there exist a coherent code of rights in EC law. This deficit may in part have led the European Council meeting in Cologne in June 1999 to decide to create a Charter to make the overriding importance and relevance of human rights 'more visible to the Union's citizens', and to set up a drafting Convention to draw up the Charter.

The Charter is intended by many governments to improve the protection of rights throughout the Union by enhancing public awareness of our basic rights, and to narrow the gap between the individual citizen and the rather remote institutions of the Union. However, public awareness alone cannot remedy the gaps left by the absence of a coherent human rights code. This key point was made by the Report on the EU Charter by the House of Lords Select Committee on the European Union, published in May 2000. I was privileged to serve as a member of the Sub-Committee on Law and Institutions, chaired by Lord Hope of Craighead, which wrote the report.

Our Report concluded that

'[w]hile a declaratory Charter might help to clarify the obligations of the institutions of the EU, it would not confer direct and tangible benefits on individuals', and would 'close none of the gaps that currently exist in Community law in the protection of fundamental rights'.

We took note of the plethora of existing declarations on human rights already produced by the European institutions. In the event that the Charter was made legally binding, we were concerned by the possibility of conflict and differing interpretations between the ECJ and the European Court of Human Rights. This could have the effect of undermining the authority of the Strasbourg Court and creating legal uncertainty. We concluded that accession by the EU to the ECHR remained the 'crucial step' in guaranteeing a firm and consistent foundation for human rights in Europe.

The UK Government, in its response to the Select Committee's Report took a different view, regarding the Amsterdam Treaty as an adequate legal guarantee of basic rights, and the Charter as a useful device for 'making rights more visible to the people'. There is a clear divergence here in views as to what should be the essential purpose of the Charter. Either it should be seen primarily as a showcase or set of non-binding guidelines, or an essential step in the process of closing gaps in the legal protection of human rights in the EU.

The Government does not believe that accession by the Community to the ECHR is essential. Nor does the Government accept that the UK should agree to extend full ECJ jurisdiction over the areas covered by the Third Pillar. In the Government's words in its response to the Select Committee's report,

'[...] these raise sensitive issues relating to national sovereignty – law and order and the criminal justice process. An acceptance of extended jurisdiction would have to be on a 'once and for all' basis.'

The Government points out, rather lamely, that

'[...] in any event, there is already some scope for the review or interpretation of third pillar measures by the ECJ, at the suit of the Commission or the Member States, pursuant to Article 35(6) and (7) TEU.'

That, however, provides no means of effective redress for the individual whose human rights are violated by an EU official or body in relation to activities covered by the Third Pillar.

The final draft of the Charter was published on 28 September 2000. It contains seven 'chapters' of rights. The first two chapters, on 'Dignity' and 'Freedom', set out the basic civil and political rights, often departing from the wording of such rights in the ECHR and recognising new variants of such rights, such as the freedom to conduct a business and the right of protection of personal dignity. The next chapter, on 'Equality', recognises the right to non-discrimination, gender equality, cultural, religious and linguistic diversity, and the rights of the child and the elderly. The fourth chapter, on 'Solidarity', sets out the basic socio-economic rights, in a manner that is watered down from earlier drafts of the Charter. Rights such as workers' rights to information and consultation, and the right of collective bargaining and action, are subject to 'national laws and practice', a restriction that the UK Government has insisted on in response to concerns from business organisations and the national press. The fifth chapter, on 'Citizens' Rights', sets out the basic participatory rights of EU citizens and the rights of free movement and access to services guaranteed under existing EC law. The sixth chapter, on 'Justice', sets out the basic rights to the due process of law. The seventh chapter, containing 'General Provisions', restricts the scope of the Charter to the implementation of Union law and to the institutions and bodies of the Union. Article 53 provides that nothing in this Charter shall be interpreted as restricting human rights as guaranteed by Member States, by the ECHR or international agreements to which the Member States are parties.

Much of the controversy and press comment that has surrounded the Charter has centred on the question of the inclusion and scope of socio-economic rights. The final draft has been praised by employers' associations and the UK Government for restricting the scope of these rights, which are, in the Government's words,

'[...] more in the nature of principles to inform policy-making rather than rights enjoyed by individuals.'

For this very reason, the draft Charter has been criticised by social NGOs and trade unions (see the contributions of Alhadeff and Sumner, as well as Dave Feickert in this book).

The stance one takes on socio-economic rights depends to a large extent on one's theory and understanding of the principles of democracy, including the separation of powers between the unelected judiciary, elected legislatures, and governments accountable both to the legislature and the courts. The civil and political rights contained in the ECHR and the UN International Covenant on Civil and Political Rights are recognised as being enforceable in courts throughout the EU. In contrast, socio-economic rights such as the right to a fair wage are not widely regarded as justiciable in Western democracies, and are not usually enforceable in courts. The unelected judiciary has no mandate or special expertise to make decisions about how economic and social choices are to be made in allocating public funds. The European Social Charter and the UN International Covenant on Economic, Social and Cultural Rights, by which the EU Member States are bound are not enforceable in courts of law, but are subject to non-judicial supervision.

The Report of the Lords' Select Committee expressed the view that

> '[n]o Member State or common law country to the best of our knowledge has a charter of rights which goes beyond the basic civil and political rights, apart from some limited additions dealing with discrimination and the freedom of association.'

The Report recommended that the non-legally binding nature of such rights should be made apparent on the face of the Charter and that they be put in a separate part of the Charter. The final draft does this.

Many of the contributors here (see again Alhadeff and Sumner, Andrew Duff and Dave Feickert) seek to make the case for legal enforcement of socio-economic rights. They acknowledge in the main that such enforcement can be legally problematic.

7

Any legal enforcement of socio-economic rights under EC law raises the awkward constitutional and political question in the European context as to whether the ECJ, as opposed to the Commission, Council, Parliament and the Member States, is the appropriate institution to be entrusted with making economic and social choices. The democratic deficit that exists between the individual citizen and the European institutions has been much commented upon: empowering judges to enforce social and economic goals would increase the democratic deficit by removing these political choices from elected legislatures and governments and entrusting them to unelected judges. That would surely undermine public confidence in the authority of the judiciary and would ultimately weaken the respect for the rule of law.

This is in no way to deny the fundamental importance of socio-economic rights. Dave Feickert of the TUC rightly emphasises that economic and social rights and civil and political rights are indivisible. The Charter acknowledges this by recognising the basic socio-economic rights. However, it is also sensible to limit the scope of these rights to that recognised by 'national laws and practices'. While all human rights are of fundamental importance, not all human rights should be enforced in the same manner.

What is important, is for the human rights that can be effectively enforced in the courts to be adequately recognised and protected in European law. The touchstone is the existence of adequate legal safeguards against the abuse of human rights. There is a real need to ensure that the EU institutions are bound to comply with the ECHR rights, under each of the three Pillars. As the Select Committee observed:

> 'The main function of the Charter may [...] be seen as being to improve the practical enjoyment of the fundamental rights that are already secured by the ECHR so that those rights are more effectively enjoyed by individuals within the EU [...]'.

Unfortunately, the draft Charter fails to achieve this. It is purely declaratory and its declarations are couched in the ambiguous language of political compromise.

Professor Piet Eeckhout suggests that the Charter will provide courts with a road map, in place of the 'mere compass' which they possess now, with the eventual result that in terms of legal practice the charter will shape the jurisprudence of the ECJ and other courts. However, as he notes, this will not remove the ambivalence and uncertainty that will inevitably surround a purely declaratory document. Nor will this serve to clarify the uncertain relationship between the EU and the ECHR.

The Charter should not seek to 'update' the protection given by the ECHR: as Lord Goldsmith QC says, this would be to underestimate the dynamic nature of the ECHR. Nor should the Charter leave open the question of the relationship between the ECJ and the European Court of Human Rights: the ECJ should be required to 'take into account' the jurisprudence of the Strasbourg Court, in the same was as British courts are obliged to have regard to the ECHR case-law when interpreting and applying the Human Rights Act 1998.

Michael Meehan notes that the Charter represents 'uncharted waters' for the EU:

'The relationship between the EU and the ECHR needs to be reassessed and the creation of a hierarchy of rights standards with different enforcement mechanisms and content would be a threat to both the consistency and effectiveness of rights protection within Europe'.

I remain convinced that the best way of enhancing the effective European protection of human rights would be by enabling the EU to accede to the ECHR. Lord Russell-Johnston, in his contribution to this book, emphasises that there is no final external appeal to a non-EU court to determine the compatibility of EU acts with the ECHR or other international human rights standards. The crucial importance of this step has become lost in the controversy surrounding the inclusion of socio-economic rights in the Charter and the dispute as to its legal status. As noted by Jackie Gower in her contribution, most candidate countries advocate this as a first step, as they are conscious of the importance of the ECHR and its role in surrounding countries, such as the Ukraine, which may not enter the EU for decades.

Jonathan Cooper and Róisín Pillay from JUSTICE identify the central issue that has been lost sight of in the Charter debates.

'The crucial question about the Charter is not whether it can or will be used for unacknowledged political purposes, but how far it can achieve the objective of any human rights instrument, and the objective cited in the preamble to the current draft Charter: enhancing the protection of fundamental rights […]. The first and essential aim of the Charter must be to ensure that basic civil and political rights are given sufficient protection within the EU […]. Whatever the status of the Charter, it should be viewed as a step towards ECHR accession, rather than as a substitute for it.'

Political rhetoric must not be allowed to obscure what is necessary for the effective protection of the basic rights of the European citizen against infringements by the European institutions and their officials.

It is a matter of regret that the political energy that has been devoted to the Charter has not also been directed to the urgent need to provide additional help for the new European Court of Human Rights to enable it to cope with the vast burdens that threaten the effectiveness of the ECHR system. The new Court is struggling to deal with an ever-increasing case load from 41 countries in some 27 European languages. The premature entry of the Russian Federation into the ECHR system is aggravating the serious problems resulting from the expansion of the Court's work in the aftermath of the collapse of the Soviet Empire. Without the support of the old European Commission of Human Rights, the new Court is the sole institution to decide questions of admissibility, to establish the relevant facts, and to give binding and authoritative judgements. So far its success has been impressive, as has been the quality of its judgements - testimony to the skill and dedication of the judges of the Court and their staff. However, unless the Court is given additional help, the entire ECHR system will begin to decay. That is surely a more pressing concern than the signing of a declaratory Charter.

That is not to say that the Charter debate is unimportant, but only that it is less important than what is needed for the rescue of the European Court of Human Rights from its increasing plight. I am sceptical about the practical value of a purely declaratory Charter, but I commend this book to everyone who is concerned to understand the issues at stake in the current debate and beyond.

Chapter 1

TOWARDS A EUROPEAN FEDERAL SOCIETY

Andrew Duff

Reflecting the position of the European Parliament in and on the Convention, this chapter puts the Charter in the wider context of European integration. It stresses the importance of developing a consistent and comprehensive rights regime at EU level for checking, legitimising and consolidating the increasingly powerful system of European government and clarifying the relationship between the EU and its citizens by enhancing their individual rights. To contribute to the definition of the EU's identity and underlying values and rights the Charter needs to be incorporated into the EU Treaty and have binding legal effect. Potential conflicts with national constitutions and the ECHR's legal system are addressed and options for their resolution are advanced in order to avoid concerns about the Charter becoming an instrument for the unlawful extension of EU competences as well as about the emergence of two competing jurisdictions for the protection of fundamental rights in Europe.

Although it is now impossible to consider how our lives would be without the European Union, it is curious that an organisation that has achieved such an important permanence should yet be so undermined by misunderstanding and controversy. As it faces its fifth and biggest round of enlargement, some fundamental reflection about the origins of the Union, its present state and future purpose is in order.

This desirable period of political reflection takes several forms, including the drafting of the new Treaty of Nice. The Charter of Fundamental Rights should be seen in this context. It is not a new idea. Individual rights have been regarded as an integral part of the development of the modern European polity since at least Locke and Montesquieu. Rights comprise the sinews for the social contract between government and the people, which, since 1945, has had to stretch beyond the tight confines of national state boundaries. Federalists, notably Altiero Spinelli in the Draft Treaty adopted by the European Parliament in 1984, have long argued that a transnational constitutional pact would require at its core a Bill of Rights.

Many of us have been nervous at the precipitate emergence of federal authority at the EU level without a commensurate success in our efforts to develop a European federal society. Being unable to command much of a popular loyalty, the European Union institutions as presently constituted are fairly unstable. More social legitimisation is badly required to complement the Union's formal political legitimacy, for European unification without vibrant liberal democracy would be neither desirable nor permanent.

Nervousness about how authority is exercised within the Union has been accentuated by the prospect of the next enlargement, which will include states that have only a weak or, at any rate, a short liberal democratic tradition. As recently as 1990 in some of the Central European countries now negotiating accession to the EU, state control was the predominant feature and imperative in almost all aspects of life; the people were deemed to serve the state, and not the state the people. The general experience of most candidate countries, indeed, has been the antithesis of that of the West European countries that have so far made up the membership of the Union, despite the fact that both unreconstructed communism and neo-fascism continues to infect Western political society to some degree.

None of us, wiser now for the history of the twentieth century, should be complacent about how the exercise of power may jeopardise human rights. As Europe's integration continues at a fast pace, it is surely prudent before the next enlargement to develop a rights regime at the supranational level of the European Union. The proposed Charter of Fundamental Rights will help us create that elusive European public space whose politics will serve to check, legitimate and consolidate the new system of European government.

The role of rights in European integration

Best to start our fundamental reflection on the state of Europe by reminding ourselves what the European Union is for. It was conceived as one of several initiatives to ensure that Europe did not descend again into Nazi barbarism. The Charter of the United Nations in 1948 and the 1950 European Convention for the Protection of Human Rights and Fundamental Freedoms (ECHR) of the Council of Europe were drawn up by most of the very same people (saving the British) who went on to found the original European Community as the solid core of European integration. The Preamble to the Treaty of Rome (1957) speaks of the resolution of the Member States 'by thus pooling their resources to preserve and strengthen peace and liberty'. By entrenching a duty to solidarity, the European Community sought to enshrine the fundamental right of its citizens to a peaceable order. The Maastricht Treaty (1992) says that the European Union's

'task shall be to organise, in a manner demonstrating consistency and solidarity, relations between the Member States and between their peoples' (Article 1 TEU).

The Amsterdam Treaty (1997) asserted that the Union

'is founded on the principles of liberty, democracy, respect for human rights and fundamental freedoms, and the rule of law' (Article 6 (1) TEU), as well as, in the Preamble, confirming attachment to fundamental social rights as defined in the European Social Charter of 1961 and the 1989 Community Charter of the Fundamental Social Rights of Workers.

It is not surprising that social rights feature strongly in the Union's canon because one of its top political and economic objectives was to enable the free movement of workers and, later, of all its peoples between Member States. Discrimination on the grounds of nationality was prohibited from the outset (Article 12 TEC), and, after Amsterdam, the Union was empowered to

> '[...] take appropriate action to combat discrimination based on sex, racial or ethnic origin, religion or belief, disability, age or sexual orientation' (Article 13 TEC).

Both within the Treaties that bind the Union institutions and Member States together and in the jurisprudence of the European Court of Justice (ECJ), the recognition of the need to enforce observance of fundamental rights for the citizen of the European Union has grown. The Treaty of Amsterdam even goes so far as to allow membership of the Union to be suspended in the case of a 'serious and persistent breach' of human rights (Article 7 TEU).

So individual rights and the need to enforce them have featured strongly in Europe's post-war process of 'ever closer union', and they have done so increasingly as the scale and scope of integration has spread. Nevertheless, the current situation with regard to fundamental rights is unsatisfactory in at least three respects. First, the rights regime of the European Union is inconsistent in terms of content as well as variable in terms of implementation and levels of enforcement between Member States. For example, although one feature common to all Member States is the ECHR, by no means have all the Convention's subsequent protocols been signed or ratified by all Member States. In the field of social policy, the variable

16

application of the conventions of the Council of Europe and the International Labour Organisation is yet more marked.

Second, although the European Union

'[...] shall respect fundamental rights, as guaranteed by the ECHR and as they result from the constitutional traditions common to the Member States, as general principles of Community law' (Article 6(2) TEU),

it is in an anomalous situation with respect to its Member States because the Union is not itself a signatory of the Convention. The Court of Justice has confirmed that as the Treaty stands the Union is not competent to become a signatory of the ECHR. The current Intergovernmental Conference (IGC) can and should rectify this matter. Arguments about Union competence should not be allowed to get in the way of action to prevent a deterioration of human rights in Europe. The European Union needs a human rights policy to combat racism and xenophobia, to improve the treatment of refugees, and to eliminate vicarious discrimination.

Third, the steady but complex development of European integration over fifty years has left the relationship between the citizen and the European Union authorities somewhat lacking in clarity and precision. The European Parliament, in its resolution on the Charter of 16 March 2000, has affirmed its support for the federalist contention that a consolidation of the rights of the citizen will enhance the democratic legitimacy of the Union. MEPs want the constitutionalisation of the Treaties so that people will know more clearly how they are now governed, and by whom. The Charter is a necessary building block, even a corner stone, of that constitutional settlement. The Parliament believes that a mandatory Charter, with binding effect upon the European Union, will insure the citizen against an abuse of the large concentration of power that now resides at the level of the Union.

Competence and subsidiarity

So the Charter is needed. But how far should it go?

In the Roman tradition, rights exist only by virtue of law. Rights can be permissive (by granting liberties), immunity (by offering protection), prohibitive (by imposing duties and impediments) or procedural (by regulating the legal system). The Charter will need to establish coherence and interdependence between all these types of rights, and consistency between the internal and external stance of the Union. Accordingly, the Convention set up to draft the Charter has sought to focus on rights where legal remedy can be supplied; and while it has made statements about principles, it has avoided cataloguing policy aspirations.

The hard-working Convention has also been much concerned to focus on the existing powers of the European Union, and not to extend them inadvertently. Still less has the Convention plotted to by-pass the parallel work of the IGC in considering new Union competences.

The application of the principle of subsidiarity to the drafting of the Charter implies non-interference in the relationship between national citizens and their own state authorities in matters that do not concern the implementation of EU law and policy. However, in practice such rigid distinctions are difficult to draw in the European Union. Powers and responsibilities are more often shared between the EU level and Member State governments than they are delegated exclusively to the EU institutions. There is no right of general competence for the EU. All efforts to establish a definitive catalogue of federal competences are likely to be in vain, either because of the inherent instability of the state of integration or because of insurmountable differences of interpretation between Member States entrenched in their own national constitutional traditions.

The fact is that the principle of subsidiarity does not sit easily alongside the concept of fundamental rights. Whereas, on the one hand, it is legitimate for the drafters of the Charter to take cognisance of subsidiarity, it is also legitimate to argue that subsidiarity should take its place only as one of several general principles that guide the Union. Subsidiarity should not be regarded as an overriding constraint on the central powers of the Union; nor should it be elevated beyond its station to become an impediment to the fundamental nature of a European Union rights regime. The struggles of the Convention over this dilemma have produced a fairly pragmatic result.

Controversy over the application of the principle of subsidiarity has been greatest in the social field. Some in the Convention have argued for a more extensive reflection of social policy, including, for example, a fundamental right to good housing. But as the Treaty stands at present, to guarantee such a 'right' would be the duty of Member States. The European Union is not competent in housing policy in the sense that it could offer legal remedies to the homeless. The same applies to the jobless, where the Union currently only has the power to encourage high levels of employment. The treatment of its own *fonctionnaires* apart, the Union has no existing competence to set wage policy or to regulate strikes.

The Parliament believes, nevertheless, that the Charter should fully reflect the importance of the social dimension of the activities of the Union, including the centrality of social cohesion to its economic policy orientations. The right to strike and comparable rights in the field of social welfare are very much part of the social democratic tradition of all EU Member States, and they can therefore be safely assumed by the Convention and written down in the Charter without, we feel, subverting the Treaty. Besides, the single market has implications for social policy that are not yet legislated for successfully at the EU level, such as consultation of workers.

The importance of mandatory effect

The European Union is not a state but a powerful union of states exercising authority over people whose rights deserve credible and comprehensive protection. For this reason, the Parliament insists that the Charter should be included eventually within the Treaty on European Union so that it should have legal effect upon the institutions and agencies of the European Union - including Member States when and in so far as they carry out EU law and policy.

There are various ways in which incorporation into the Treaty could be achieved, and each would have a different legal effect, at least in the short term. One obvious option would be to establish the Charter as a Protocol to Article 6 of the Treaty on European Union. The Parliament will return to this issue when it considers whether or not to grant its assent to the draft Charter in the autumn.

MEPs can see no real benefit in a Charter of Rights which merely proclaims an existing set of rights. Indeed, we fear that the public may be rather cynical about the publication of yet another piece of Euro-rhetoric, however stylish and well-meaning. A non-binding Charter would also have little relevance for candidate or third countries in informing their relations with the Union.

Furthermore, a Charter that was a non-binding declaration would fail to resolve one of the existing serious contradictions in the constitutional development of the European Union. The Union would be laying claim to the existence of fundamental rights at Union level, yet in striking breach of the constitutional traditions of Member States that it is pledged to uphold, it would not be installing a concomitant legal remedy. Due process of judicial review and the capacity to seek redress is an integral part of the rights regimes of Member States. Do we really want the Union to be less than the sum of its parts in respect of citizens' rights? That is why the Convention has proceeded on the presumption that the Charter could have a mandatory character.

The Parliament has also been anxious to ensure the closest possible collaboration between the work of the Convention and the IGC. A binding Charter will require several adjustments to be made to the Treaty as well as other, sub-Treaty, reforms, not least as far as the Court of Justice is concerned.

That the ECJ will become competent in human rights issues offers the prospect of a more expeditious form of judgement than that which is possible under current procedures at the European Court of Human Rights. If the Charter is to be justiciable by the Court of Justice, Article 230 TEC will need to be given a more flexible interpretation in order to improve the individual access of the EU citizen to the Court. Treaty amendment is needed to reclassify the EU citizen as a privileged litigant: Article 34 ECHR concerning individual applications may be a model. In any case, urgent changes to the working methods of the Court and an increase in its resources will be absolutely necessary to ensure the smooth and speedy administration of justice in more case-work over a wider field.

No regression

The Charter must not reduce the rights of any existing citizen by undermining the ECHR. On the contrary, it should expressly safeguard the existing human rights *acquis* of each Member State, after the manner of Article 53 of the ECHR, while not diluting the important general principle of European Community law concerning uniformity of application. The Charter must maximise legal certainty in all cases. The European Parliamentary delegation in the Convention has been insistent on this point.

The European Council has rightly proposed a Charter of the *Union*. As the Treaty of Amsterdam is brought into effect, and as the international profile of the Union continues to grow, the distinction between the First 'Community-method' Pillar of Maastricht and the Second and Third 'intergovernmental' Pillars becomes increasingly academic. Convergence between the three would be the natural consequence of a more comprehensive and co-ordinated approach to integration by all concerned. The distinction of the pillars is not, at any rate, appreciated by the citizen, for whom, no doubt, a single Charter of Rights covering the whole spectrum of EU activity would make sense. This is also true for foreign companies operating inside the EU, for whom the Charter may have some profound implications.

Moreover, many of the most sensitive questions concerning fundamental rights lie in the Second and Third Pillars. The effective incarnation of a common European security and defence policy poses new challenges for the Union in the field of ethics, in the behaviour of EU representatives abroad, and in the treatment of foreign nationals. Progress towards common asylum and immigration policies promotes new categories of legitimate minorities within the Union. And developments in co-operation between Member State police and judicial authorities, such as the creation of Europol and the incorporation of the Schengen Agreement within the Treaty on European Union, have a potentially dramatic impact on the relationship between the EU institutions and its agencies on the one hand and the citizen on the other.

The European Parliament believes that fundamental rights are indivisible and interdependent, and that it would be crazy to connive in allowing two competing legal systems to develop for the protection of fundamental rights according to whether the measures at issue were covered by the EC Treaty (crossing external borders, asylum, immigration, legal co-operation in civil matters) or by the Treaty on European Union (criminal matters). Therefore, notwithstanding the different mix of competences between Member States and institutions according to policy area and legal base, we are reinforced in our view that the Charter must embrace the whole work of the Union. This implies that the Union itself must obtain legal personality - a proposal the Parliament has indeed put to the IGC.

Relationship with the Council of Europe

The accession of the European Community to the European Convention on Human Rights has been under discussion for many years. The launching of the Charter adds new urgency to that debate, for it is clear already that the ECHR is to form the solid core of the Charter. In order to guarantee scrupulous respect of the ECHR and to overcome the current anomalous position of the EU institutions, the European Parliament believes that the Union itself should sign up to and ratify the ECHR and all its protocols. As the Court of Justice has proposed (*Opinion 2/94*), this requires Treaty amendment in order to obtain full legal personality for the European Union. The Union should not seek to become a member of the Council of Europe but, merely, a High Contracting Party to the ECHR. In this way problems of dual representation and the participation of the Union in the political organs of the Council could be avoided.

There is some understandable disquiet about the potential for conflict and duplication between the European Court of Justice in Luxembourg and the European Court of Human Rights in Strasbourg. However, under Article 32(2) of the ECHR in the event of any dispute as to whether the Strasbourg Court has jurisdiction, it is that Court that shall decide. Article 55 (ECHR) precludes other means of dispute settlement except by special agreement. Such an arrangement would be required to square the obligations of signing the ECHR with Article 292 TEC, in which Member States undertake not to submit a dispute concerning the interpretation or application of the Treaty to any third party method of settlement.

The Treaty of Amsterdam has already granted the ECJ competence over human rights issues (Article 46 TEU). The Luxembourg Court is certainly capable of developing its own jurisprudence in human rights issues, as national courts have done, while recognising the authority of Strasbourg in the last resort. The risk of duplication with Strasbourg can be minimised by respecting Article 35(2)(b) ECHR, which states that the Strasbourg Court will decline the admissibility of applications that have

'[...] already been submitted to another procedure of international investigation or settlement and contains no relevant new information'.

The roles of the Council of Europe's Court of Human Rights and the EU's Court of Justice are different. Strasbourg does not have the trappings of a federal supreme court; but Luxembourg, which does, will have to accept the authority of the former where the ECHR is implicated in the same way that it has accepted the arbitration of the WTO in trade disputes, and as national judiciaries have also been able to do. We await with interest the outcome of the negotiation of a protocol between the two Courts that is intended to manage their transverse relationship.

The ECHR, while universal in its application to individuals, is likely to remain more restricted in substantive terms than that of the EU Charter. Not only will the latter bear upon special categories of rights for EU citizens and resident foreigners, but it is also likely to be more egalitarian and progressive in its formulation of certain rights in civic, social, environmental and other fields. In that the ties that bind Member States of the European Union are much tighter than those that commit the more numerous Member States of the Council of Europe, the EU Charter is bound to have a wider scope than that of the ECHR. For example, whereas Protocol No. 4 of the ECHR lays down the right to move freely *within* and to *leave* its signatory states, the EU Charter will seek to give effect to the right to freedom of movement and residence *between* its Member States.[1]

Boost to political reform

Writing constitutions is usually easier than revising them afterwards, so the IGC would be prudent to adopt provisions for amending the Charter. The Parliament has welcomed the innovation of the Convention as a superior method of working to that of the IGC itself. We would support - but insist upon - a repeat of this exercise to supplement or limit the Charter in the future. Similarly, no act of the Commission or Council to derogate from the Charter should be admissible without the Parliament's agreement.

Although the Charter will not redistribute competences between the Union and its Member States, which can only be done by Treaty amendment, it will doubtless stretch the interpretation of the powers with which the EU is endowed. The Charter will have a gradual and determined effect on the quality of integration, articulated via jurisprudence of the ECJ and by informing the actions of the political institutions. The installation of binding rights at the heart of the Treaty will shift the paradigms of European integration by elevating the role of the citizen in contradistinction to those of the institutions and Member States. To that extent, the Charter should certainly be welcomed by all those who seek the further political reform of the Union.

Parliament has wanted the Charter to be ambitious, and to write down in Treaty form modern fundamental civil and social rights as well as to reiterate rights well established elsewhere. Although some MEPs will criticise the evident self-restraint of the Convention, a broad cross-party majority accept that the Charter's purpose is not to compensate for legislative shortcomings in all and sundry policy areas. The Parliament as a whole is likely to be fairly well pleased by the final draft which promises to establish for the sake of the citizen that the Union fully respects and guarantees modern standards of fundamental rights in those areas where it is competent to do so.

It should be stressed that the European Parliament does not see the Charter as an attempt to subvert the existing constitutional order of Member States, but, rather, to strengthen the identity of the European Union. The Charter will contribute to the definition of the collective patrimony of values and rights which bind Europeans together and underpin all the Union's policies. It will sharpen the profile of the Union in terms of democracy, social justice, ecology and human rights. The Charter will do that, even if it effectively raises the eventual threshold of membership. MEPs, at least, are clear-headed about the Charter's role in the process of preparing the Union for enlargement.

Given the relative success of the Convention in its weighty drafting process, the European Parliament is likely to approve the final draft. This will mean that the Charter can be 'proclaimed' at Nice. But MEPs will not be satisfied with a mere proclamation. They would be wise to insist on a firm Treaty-based commitment by the IGC to integrate the Charter within a constitutional treaty at an early future date.

Notes

[1] Another example: whereas the EU Charter will insist on a general prohibition of discrimination on the grounds of gender, Article 14 ECHR only pertains to sex discrimination in relation to the other rights of the Convention.

Chapter 2

Consolidation of Fundamental Rights at EU Level – the British Perspective

Lord Goldsmith

This chapter argues that it has become increasingly necessary to constrain the powers of the EC legislators and administrators by the obligation to respect fundamental rights. The Charter is therefore intended to be a proclamation of existing rights showing the limits on the powers of the Union institutions. Reflecting the position of the UK government as well as the discussions in the Convention, it is emphasised that the Charter's scope does neither extend to Member States acting in their areas of national competence nor does it give the EU new competences. The Charter is not seen as an instrument for creating new rights or an embryo Constitution for a Federal States of Europe. It shall also not create a parallel system of fundamental rights protection in competition with the ECHR. Regarding economic and social rights, the Charter should not include mere political objectives which the EU cannot deliver and which are therefore best decided upon in a national legislative context. The reference in the draft text to 'principles' which amount to enforceable rights only where implemented by national law, according to the respective national practices, or, where there is such a competence, by EC law, is presented as a good solution.

I would like, in this Chapter, to discuss some of the aspects of the work of the Convention on the drafting of the Charter of Fundamental Rights and particularly the approach to the rights contained in it. We write before the final meetings of the Convention; the final text of the Charter is not settled nor is it certain that there will be a text which achieves consensus as our mandate, settled at the European Council Meetings in Cologne and Tampere last year, requires. So there will have to be elements of uncertainty in what I write. The reader will have to be understanding about that.

Why the Charter?

The first question, which needs to be asked, and answered, is what the purpose of the Charter is. This is critical. It is important to explain what the content of the Charter should contain and what its status and effect will be.

To answer this question it is desirable, I believe, to put the issue in the historical context of the development of the European Union.

The period after the Second World War saw the emergence of the great building blocks for the protection of human rights which had been so profoundly violated in the immediately preceding years: the creation of the United Nations whose Charter is explicitly founded on the reaffirmation of 'faith in fundamental human rights and in the dignity and worth of the human person'; the beginnings of a global system of international human rights law (which had never existed before) of which the Universal Declaration of Human Rights followed later by the two binding United Nations' Covenants are the best known, but by no means the only examples; and the protection of human rights at the regional level. In Europe, the Council of Europe, and its proud jewel, the European Convention of Human Rights put into practice a vigorous and imaginative judicial system for the protection of the fundamental rights of individuals against the power of the State.

Yet, despite these events which were happening at the very time of the birth of the European Communities, the founding Treaties made no mention of fundamental rights. As the focus of the Treaties was economic integration this may not be surprising. It would not have seemed that Treaties would be operating in areas or by methods which were inherently likely to violate human rights. But as the competence and the law-making of the Communities have grown, the need became greater for an explicit recognition at the Union level of the rights of citizens of the Union (and others living within its protection). The Communities and other institutions and bodies were not directly bound, as were the Member States, by the terms of the European Convention of Human Rights because the Communities were not parties, unlike the Member States, to the European Convention. So the idea began to be developed that the powers of the Community's legislators and administrators needed to be constrained in the way that the legislators and administrators of the Member States are constrained by a clearly spelt out obligation to respect fundamental rights.

The Court of Justice was the first to develop this idea, recognising through its jurisprudence that certain fundamental freedoms were to be recognised as general principles of community law which the Communities were obliged to respect. Finding those principles was at that stage for the Court to do; though it accorded a special place of importance for the ECHR.

The Member States followed this up at Maastricht by including for the first time in the Treaty (what is now Article 6(2) TEU) an explicit recognition of the concept of fundamental rights and an obligation on the Union institutions to respect those fundamental rights guaranteed by the ECHR and deriving from the constitutional traditions common to Member States.

However, apart from the reference to the ECHR, the Treaty did not set out a clear catalogue of what those fundamental freedoms are. This leaves vague and unclear for the citizen what the rights are that he or she can expect to be respected at the Union level and it leaves uncertainty as to what the rights are that the ECJ is expected to enforce.

This is the background against which the decision of the European Council at Cologne is to be viewed. That decision was to draw up a declaration of existing rights enjoyed by EU citizens concluding that

> '[a]t the present stage of the development of the European Union, the fundamental rights applicable at Union level should be consolidated in a Charter and thereby made more evident.'

The purpose of the Charter, as conceived, was therefore to make the existing rights which the Union ought to respect more visible. To my mind, that was for two reasons. First, the purpose is to deepen and strengthen the culture of rights and responsibilities in the EU. Bringing together into a single document endorsed by the Member States and Community institutions a proclamation of existing rights will have a powerful effect in reinforcing in the minds of administrators, governments and legislators the rights that citizens possess and the need to respect them. The second purpose is to remedy this lack of clarity in the protection of human rights by declaring clearly which are the rights the Union is to respect. Its purpose in this respect is to restrain the powers of the Union, by showing the areas in which it must not trample on the rights of the citizens when exercising the powers it has.

The clear position repeatedly taken by the UK government, as by others, is that achievement of this purpose is best attained through a strong and clear political declaration rather than through a legally binding text. But this issue is not one for the Convention to decide. The mandate makes it clear that, once we have finished our job, it will be for the Member States to decide 'whether, and if so how, to integrate the Charter into the Treaties'. So the Charter drafters will have to sit back and watch that decision being made.

The scope and status of the Charter

From that understanding of the purpose of the Charter, a number of elements of the Charter and its scope and status become clear.

First, the principal addressees of the Charter are the European Union institutions when acting in the sphere of their competences and not the Member States when acting in areas within national competence. It is the EU institutions which legislate at the Union level. The purpose of the Charter is to show the limits on the powers which the Union has when exercising the competences provided under the Treaties. It is the EU institutions which are not already clearly bound, unlike Member States, to respect a clear catalogue of fundamental rights set out in the European Convention or in a national constitution. It is for them, therefore, that the Charter is intended. Member States are not the addressees except to the limited extent that they are acting in the implementation of Community or Union law. When they are acting in this capacity they are really acting as the agents of the Community to implement the law passed and so naturally will be subject to the same constraints. But in the areas of national competence, the Charter is not intended to affect Member States. In those areas, the protection of fundamental freedoms for the citizen will be the existing structure of national law and constitution and important international obligations like the European Convention on Human Rights. In the United Kingdom that will particularly mean, from October of this year, the Human Rights Act. This is critical. For example, without this understanding each state would otherwise have had to insist on the Charter simply mirroring what is in its own national constitution, as it could not accept either greater or lesser obligations in its own national dealings with its people.

This limitation on the scope of the Charter will be very clear from the text. The existing draft Article 50 therefore makes clear that '[t]he provisions of this Charter are addressed to the institutions and bodies of the Union with due regard for the principle of subsidiarity and to the Member States only when they are implementing Union law.'

So the Charter will not impose on Member States any obligation when they are acting within their areas of national competence. Still less will it enable the European Court of Justice to rule on acts taken within purely national competence by Member States. This will be important, for example, in many of the areas which relate to the social and economic field which are essentially for national governments, elected by the people, rather than judges, to determine.

Secondly, the Charter is not an exercise in extending the competence of the European Union. The purpose of the Charter is not to give Brussels new powers or tasks but to limit those powers by making clear the restrictions on what they do - emphasising that they cannot trample on fundamental rights of citizens in doing so. The Charter will make this clear also. So the present draft declares that

'[t]his Charter does not establish any new power or task for the Community or the Union, or modify powers and tasks defined by the Treaties.'

This is an important limitation which has often not been understood in public comment on the Charter as it has been progressed. It is the answer to those critics who see the Charter as a way of taking more powers to Brussels and away from national governments. That is not what it will do. What is now for national governments to decide will be the same after the Charter is agreed as it was before. The Charter will not change that position.

Thirdly, the exercise is not about minting new rights. It is an exercise, the United Kingdom Government firmly believes, in increasing the visibility of existing rights. That much is clear from the Cologne Conclusions. They were not a mandate to create new rights. There is an established procedure for creating new rights at EU level. That is through directives and other legislative instruments adopted by processes in which each of the institutions plays its role as do, where appropriate, the social partners. Despite the innovative structure of the Convention, which has provided a great transparency to the work of drafting, the working methods necessarily adopted for the body, the very short period of time in which we have been given to work and the enormous breadth of the project, would have made it impossible to engage in the detailed process of crafting genuinely new rights. Our task of identifying and describing existing fundamental rights has been difficult enough.

This issue has been more controversial within the Convention although the position explained has been strongly supported. But many non-governmental organisations have made contributions and sought inclusions plainly with the understanding that the Convention was in the business of making new rights. The Charter, as it emerges, may therefore disappoint them. But it will only do so because they have not had it clearly explained that this was not the aim of the exercise. For my part, I would have liked to see clearer explanations of this at an earlier stage so that expectations were not raised and then dashed.

Fourth, it is worth also scotching one idea which has gained some currency outside the Convention. The Charter is not a secret embryo Constitution for a Federal States of Europe. There are, of course, people throughout Europe with a federalist ambition. But the Convention has not been engaged in the job of producing any blueprint for any such exercise.

The contents of the Charter

Three baskets of rights were evident from the mandate of the Charter body: classic civil and political rights as contained in the ECHR, citizenship rights deriving from the Treaties and social and economic rights. Negotiating the contents of the

Charter has been a long and difficult process, particularly in relation to the first and third categories. There have been different points of view, different legal traditions and different political opinions. The end result will inevitably be something of a compromise but there are several elements which merit special mention.

Relationship with the ECHR

It follows from the consideration of the purpose of the Charter that it is not to replace the European Convention on Human Rights. That Convention, the most important element in the protection of human rights in Europe, both within and outside the European Union, will continue in existence and continue to apply day in and day out to the rights of many millions of people. The Charter has to contain the ECHR rights, the classic civil and political freedoms, but it will not be a substitute for them.

A major topic of debate within the Convention has therefore been the relationship with the ECHR rights which should be reflected in the Charter. At the time of writing that particular debate has not been concluded and division on this issue may yet prevent the Charter from being accepted.

The UK's position has been that the relationship with the ECHR rights should be very close. The Charter should not be a rewrite of the Convention. The Conclusions of Cologne state that the Charter 'should contain the fundamental rights and freedoms as well as basic procedural rights' guaranteed by the ECHR. Article 6(2) TEU also refers specifically to those rights. The Convention will continue to apply to all Member States and frequently be applied in the national courts. Whilst promoting the visibility of rights, we must preserve legal certainty. The ECHR is now underpinned by decades of Strasbourg case-law interpreting it. We should not unpick that. The last thing citizens need is competing versions and interpretations of fundamental rights. The rights defined in the ECHR and interpreted by the Human Rights Court should not be undermined.

In my view, this means the Charter should avoid inconsistency with the ECHR in the areas which it covers. That does not prevent other rights from being included in the Charter but, in the field which the Convention covers, the rights should be the same. The risk otherwise is of a reduction in the protection of human rights and not a strengthening. We should not therefore be appearing to create a parallel and competing system of human rights protection in the areas of the freedoms covered by the ECHR. As the President of the European Court of Human Rights noted in a speech on 7 March 2000:

> 'The Court's main concern in the context of this discussion is to avoid a situation in which there are alternative, competing and potentially conflicting systems of human rights protection both within the Union and in the greater Europe. The duplication of protection systems runs the risk of weakening the overall protection offered and undermining legal certainty in this field.'

Some have argued, however, that the ECHR should be updated, that the language is 50 years out of date. That underestimates the dynamic nature of the ECHR. It is a 'living document' which is developed all the time by the Strasbourg Court in the light of contemporary standards and to deal with modern issues. So the Court has dealt, for example, with issues of environmental protection, of non-traditional families and their right to respect, and of sexual orientation in public and private life.

So I believe we need to avoid the risk of producing competing systems, or even apparently competing systems which will provide work for lawyers, excuses for administrators but no protection for the individual. There are different methods of achieving the necessary degree of consistency with the ECHR. The language does not need to be identical if it is otherwise clear that the rights are the same. This could be done by a clear general article saying as much or by a clear definition of the relevant rights as being the same as in the ECHR, whether in the same document or even in an accompanying text.

Social and economic rights

Another area of difficulty in the Convention has been the proper treatment of social and economic rights. The Cologne Conclusions required account to be taken of these rights and referred to the two European Social Charters dealing with these topics although subject to the reservation that the Charter should avoid matters which were no more than mere objectives for action by the Union.

There are important differences to classic civil and political rights. First, social and economic rights are usually not justiciable individually in the same way as other rights. Rather they inform policy-making by the legislator. Secondly, these are 'rights' which are recognised and given effect to in different ways in the Member States in whose competence this primarily lies. National governments will therefore decide, in accordance with national priorities and the expressions of political will through the ballot box how to implement these principles and, especially, how to allocate available resources to them. To include such 'rights' alongside classic rights which are individually justiciable would create confusion and concern. At the very least it would raise expectations that the Charter is giving rights which the EU, the principal addressee, is in no position to deliver, having neither the competence nor the budget. At worst, it would actually encourage courts to substitute their judgement on what are essentially political matters for the decisions of elected governments.

Recognition of those difficulties led to much debate in the Convention as to how to deal with the issue. A number of points of view were advanced. The ultimate solution to this problem emerged as a recognition of these differences through a new concept, namely that these rights essentially take the form of principles, which, whilst common to Member States, are implemented differently in their national laws and practices; and that the principles only give rise to rights to the extent that they are implemented by national law or, in those areas where there is such competence, by Community law.

Expressing these 'rights' therefore as principles tied to national law or (where it exists) Community law provides the possibility of identifying these important areas as the ones where the Union institutions (where they do act within their fields of competence) should not act in their violation. It does not, however, provide any mandate for the Union institutions themselves to try and implement those rights, outside their own competences, or to impose on Member States some obligation to recognise the principles differently from how they do under national law.

The process of drafting to achieve this result is delicate and negotiations continue at the time of writing.

Citizenship rights

The area of citizenship rights derived from the Treaties has produced less controversy. Here, the position accepted in the Charter is that the Convention has no ability to amend the Treaties and that, therefore, the Charter is a catalogue of those rights which are fundamental but that, as the draft text provides, those rights 'shall be exercised under the conditions and within the limits defined by [the EU and EC Treaties]'.

Conclusion

I remain of the view that the Charter is capable of being a real benefit to the peoples of Britain and Europe by giving them for the first time a clear statement of the rights which the Union institutions are obliged to respect as they go about their business. The risk of creating confusion or uncertainty in the field of fundamental rights, undoing our national decisions on the right balance in economic and social affairs or the risk of impeding the Union in pursuing its other objectives, such as, for example, of achieving greater economic growth and full employment, must, however, also be considered. The text therefore has to be right. It has not been an easy task but I hope it will have been successful by the time this book comes to be read.

Chapter 3

Charter of Fundamental Rights, the Enhancement of Humans and the Curtailment of Human Rights?

Timothy Kirkhope

Starting out with some thoughts on the Human Rights Act incorporating the ECHR into domestic law, this chapter addresses the question whether the EU Charter is necessary as another parallel system of human rights protection in Europe. It is argued that the Charter can only be useful and, indeed, successful if it avoids contradictions with the ECHR. As even a declaratory Charter would have legal effects, a final appellate structure must be determined in order to avoid further confusion for national courts and European citizens. In assessing the Charter's content, it is pointed out that the inclusion of a number of social and employment rights, which go beyond the 'fundamental', is the cause of some political controversy and poses a threat to the Charter's status. Drawing on the experience on the Convention, regret is expressed that the drafting process has by some been seen as a step towards a European constitution as this is not the aim of the exercise and should be addressed in a different forum. The draft is finally criticised for failing to afford real protection to citizens against violations of their rights by the EU institutions – an opportunity lost.

The issue of human rights is one which has concerned politicians of all persuasions for many years, and in the different Members States of the European Union human rights have been treated in varying ways. In the case of the UK, there does appear to be a clear understanding by the courts, which has developed out of our common law and indeed precedent law, that cases should always take into account the human rights of the defendant or applicant, in most cases - both criminal and civil.

The previous Conservative government, although it had signed up to the Protocols of the European Convention on Human Rights which were manifested by actions of the Council of Europe as opposed to the European Union, never considered that we should incorporate the Convention into the domestic law of the United Kingdom. Subsequently this was agreed, however, under the auspices of the present Labour Government and as of 2 October 2000 the European Convention on Human Rights will be absorbed into the domestic proceedings of courts and indeed public authorities in the UK.

There are some lawyers who do not believe that this is necessary. There are other lawyers who do believe that it is necessary to have this access in domestic courts instead of just through the European Court of Human Rights, which previously alone administered these issues. They consider that there is now an opportunity for many people, who did not previously have a means of expressing their concerns regarding human rights in their own individual cases, to do so through the domestic courts in the context of the Convention on Human Rights. The decision of the European Union to proceed with the Charter of Fundamental Rights is controversial in itself for we have to decide whether or not it is necessary to have this Charter, which would give competence in human rights matters to the European Court of Justice, which in turn runs parallel with the ECHR and is not directly involved with the precedent law that emerges from the ECtHR.

There are those who are sceptical about giving the European Union powers of a legal nature, which is certainly the idea in the minds of the strongest proponents of the Charter. Also, if the Charter of Fundamental Rights does not exactly parallel the Convention on Human Rights in its provisions (and the drafts so far certainly do not), could this not create sufficient confusion that in the end will actually deny European citizens their human rights rather than enhance them? As a lawyer as well as a Conservative on the Convention, I have made it clear that these confusions, unless dealt with at an early stage, could render the whole process a negative one and the likely contradictions actually harmful to pursuing human rights.

It is, of course, now a matter for the Council of Ministers to decide if they do agree with the draft Charter handed on from the Convention to the governments of Europe. To my knowledge ten of the fifteen Member States have indicated that, whatever else happens to this Charter, it should not be given a legal base alongside the Convention on Human Rights. This would mean that the Charter could never be more than simply declaratory. However, my experience of the British courts suggests that even if it were only declaratory, they would still be obliged to take into account the contents of the Charter in determining final decisions when asked to do so by representations from applicants or defendants.

If they are also obliged to apply the terms of the Convention on Human Rights in domestic law then it is not difficult to see how much confusion will arise. One of the major elements, which has been ignored by the Convention for the Charter of Fundamental Rights, is that of determining the ultimate appellate structure, to which those who need to take an issue of this kind can have a final determination. Although there is dialogue between the European Court of Justice and the European Court of Human Rights there is no structure in place at the present time to arbitrate between the two.

Of course, it could be possible to afford to Member States the right to 'opt-in' or apply for the Charter, rather than be obliged to follow it. Applicant states waiting to join the European Union could also apply as and when they reach the criteria set down. It could be a matter of pride for them to reach that set of standards. But this is not a popular idea for the European Commission.

It is also interesting to note that the Charter of Fundamental Rights goes much further than the Convention in terms of the general area which it deems to be 'Fundamental Rights'. In the Convention on Human Rights these rights are almost exclusively dealing with, ironically, the most *fundamental* needs of the population, such matters as the right to life or the right to the freedom of expression. The Charter is supposed to be looking at fundamental rights but it actually tackles a considerable area of social and employment rights as well. Many of these might not be considered by a purist to be 'fundamental'. This apparent contradiction in itself provides political difficulties to many of us. I do not see the right vehicle for social and employment rights to be a Charter of this kind and indeed the Charter's status is seriously threatened by the determination of some people to include within it these rights.

Furthermore, there is now an opportunity to fill the vacuum where the citizens of Europe have comparatively little direct redress to the courts in Europe, about the failings and misadministration of the institutions of the European Union. Certainly the European Ombudsman has a major role and, indeed, it was the Ombudsman, in evidence given to the Convention of the Charter in the early stage, who suggested that its major role should be in relation to the protection of citizens from the institutions themselves. The Convention has failed to take that on board and as a result the one major area of concern remains an area where abuse and negligence can affect the rights of European citizens. This clearly is nonsense and a lost opportunity.

There is then the need to try and interpret the motives of some of the people supporting the Charter. There are many, who would like to see a European constitution over and above those of nation states. It is unfortunate that, if this is their motive for the Charter of Fundamental Rights, they have not stated it in an honest and straightforward manner. It is perfectly legitimate for those who believe in European integration to see the future as being one with a constitution for the whole of Europe. I, of course, have a different view. In many ways the strength of Europe, from the United Kingdom perspective, is in the nation states themselves and in the strength of the combined efforts and co-operation, which from time to time benefits all citizens of Europe. The fact that there are those with strong motives in requiring a constitution means that the Charter of Fundamental Rights is inevitably flawed. Would it not be better for those people to set about the preparation of a constitution which we can all then look at in a straightforward manner? If, as in my case, we are not happy with that, then it could be dealt with at the appropriate time and in the appropriate ways.

In conclusion, the Charter of Fundamental Rights has missed a vital opportunity to deal with the institutions of Europe. It is inevitably going to cause confusion in the courts and amongst our citizens who are trying to pursue legitimate human rights issues. There already is a vehicle in the Convention on Human Rights and the Court of Human Rights for dealing with problems of this kind. I have already expressed my view that even without the inclusion of the ECHR into domestic law there were elements of human rights protection already entrenched in the British legal system in its common law and its precedent law. We have therefore created for ourselves a new problem if it reduces, as I believe it probably will, the accessibility of the citizen to *true* human rights.

Chapter 4

A Charter of Fundamental Rights of the European Union: A Personal Political Perspective

Win Griffiths

This chapter presents a personal account of the workings of the Convention. It describes the challenges the ambiguous Cologne mandate and the restricted timetable for producing a text posed for the drafters. The Convention proceedings and the development of the draft Charter are described and the members' different positions – ranging from the minimalist to the maximalist, particularly as regards its scope and content – are explained. Despite these differences the Convention's work is judged as being constructive and successful in advancing solutions for controversial questions. It is concluded that the Charter should emphasise the rights and protection afforded to Union citizens and residents and the responsibilities of EU institutions and national governments to ensure the rule of law and good administration. The ethos of the Charter should further remind individuals of their responsibilities and guide their interpersonal relationships. Creating practical processes for the EU to promote individual and institutional rights and responsibilities is seen as a more worthwhile aim than discussing the Charter's credentials as an emerging European constitution.

When the 'body' met for the first time just before Christmas in 1999 we were in truly unchartered territory. The mandate outlined at the Cologne European Council in June was as clear and as ambiguous as the members of the 'body' wanted it to be. The large number on the 'body' - 62 decided at Tampere in the October European Council - threatened to make it unworkable. There were fears that the talking could become interminable with wide ranging debate and no decisions.

Going to the first meeting in December 1999, I felt that the European Councils of Cologne and Tampere had presented us with a more than considerable challenge to complete a draft Charter for the Council by December 2000. Within three months even this challenging timetable was speeded up with talk of the draft being ready by the end of July. (As it happened, with some additional meetings and the turning of some two-day meetings into three day sessions, a preliminary draft text (CONVENT 45) was produced before the summer break).

Throughout this process, the Secretariat and the Praesidium of the Convention – as the 'body' quickly agreed to call itself – had a mighty logistical task on its hands. The pre-preliminary draft text (CONVENTS 28 and 34) was subject to over a thousand amendments – 27 of which were mine – and it was something of a miracle that CONVENT 45 was produced by the end of July. The process had thus reached a sufficiently advanced stage for all of the substantive issues to have been well aired and negotiating positions made plain. Thus a summer of hectic activity behind the scenes was assured in order to fine-tune the July text and find a form of words to clarify the ambiguities seen by many Convention members in the Cologne mandate.

For me, the Cologne mandate was clear. The Convention was directed to consolidate in a Charter the Fundamental Rights applicable at the European Union level so that these rights, and their overriding importance, were clear to the Unions' citizens.

The Cologne mandate also directed us to the sources for setting out these rights. The Charter was to be based upon the European Convention of Human Rights, the constitutional traditions of Member States and general principles of Community law. In addition we were told to include

'[...] economic and social rights as contained in the European Social Charter and the Community Charter of Fundamental Social Rights of Workers (Article 136 TEC), insofar as they do not merely establish objectives for action by the Union'.

This latter point is at the centre of the political debate on what economic and social rights should be in the Charter, and if included, how these rights should be expressed. How, in the economic and social sector, is the judgement to be made between a 'fundamental right' and an 'objective for action by the Union'? The temptation for progressive political opinion was simply to accept that the European Social Charter and the Community Charter should be regarded as statements of fundamental rights without any attempt to decide which were desirable political objectives.

The argument continued that, as we moved into the new century and prepared for a further expansion of the European Union, this wider all-embracing view of the Charter was needed. The strongest protagonists of this view, though not exclusively, are most of the 16 Members of the European Parliament on the Convention. They see the Charter as an opportunity to strengthen the European Union and to enhance the rights of its citizens and the role of the European Parliament itself. Although to be fair to the MEP Convention members, some are prepared to distinguish between these social and economic rights which are fundamental and those which are desirable political objectives for the Union and its Member States. There are some, too, who view the exercise as an opportunity to regain for Member States some of the sovereignty they have pooled within the European Union.

The majority, however, seek a Charter that will at least be a protocol of the Treaty, though preferably a legally binding document that is incorporated into the Treaty and which covers all aspects of European Union activity, including common foreign and security policy, justice and home affairs and institutions such as Europol. Of the elected members of the Convention, the European Parliament has had the most opportunity, time and resources to develop an institutional view of the Charter. In drawing up its own report on the Charter, with rapporteurs Voggenhuber and Duff, at least six of its committees provided opinions for the Committee on Constitutional Affairs.

The 30 members of the Convention representing national parliaments broadly fall either into the maximalist view of the majority of European Parliament Members or the discerning view on social and economic rights for inclusion in the Charter. Although, here again, it would be unfair to define rigid blocks of opinion, particularly in the latter group. Non-maximalist members, such as myself, want to see rights included for children and minorities, for example, which possibly stray beyond a strict interpretation of the Cologne mandate.

A critical issue here is the nature of the Charter. The Cologne Council decision stated that the Charter was not to be a legally binding document, though at the same time it raised the possibility of the Council, at a later date, making it so. Despite there being a significant number of Convention members who would like to see the Charter legally binding rather than a declaratory document, they are, on the whole, content for the European Council to decide as laid down at Cologne. It has meant, however, and not unreasonably, that the Convention in its deliberations on the Charter has sought to draw it up in such a way as to facilitate the process for it to become legally binding.

I have always felt that this argument has had more to do with process than principle. Even though the Charter is not meant to be legally binding immediately, the fact that its purpose is to make existing rights more evident and their overriding importance and relevance more visible means that Union citizens and residents will have legal redress against the Commission and Member States when creating or implementing Community law.

Lord Goldsmith, the personal representative of the British Government, came forward with a proposal at an early stage of the proceedings to link the Charter rights clearly with their legal source in a single document with two parts: Part A stating the right and Part B its legal source. During the early stages of the Convention discussions there seemed to be in sufficient agreement to proceed along these lines though a number of members, of the maximalist school broadly speaking, did express strong reservations.

The preparatory versions up to CONVENTS 28 and 34 of the Charter have had a two-part style – but not in the way envisaged by Lord Goldsmith. A typical euro-compromise perhaps!

Late in the day - after the European Council in Feira - rumours began to circulate that the incoming French Presidency wanted to use the Charter process to develop the concept of a 'European Social Model'. This was given form in the Braibant/Meyer proposals on social and economic rights in particular. Progressive opinion had no problem with the sentiments expressed but doubts arose from two quite different angles. I felt, for example, that any rights included in the Charter had to have a legal base of some sort, either in the ECHR or in Community law, to be enforceable. On the other hand, Convention members from states like Sweden, with particularly well-developed progressive social and economic rights legislation, wanted to be reassured that, if such rights were included in the Charter, the European Court of Justice could not use the Charter as 'guidance' and possibly make decisions which would undermine national legislation in areas where Community law was not strictly applicable.

The pre-preliminary draft Charter (CONVENT 34), sought to provide re-assurance on the latter point in Article 46 by stating clearly that the Charter did not establish any new competences or modify existing ones, as defined in the Treaties, and that furthermore the Charter was addressed to the institutions and bodies of the Union and the Member States exclusively within the scope of the Treaties and Community law. These proposals were further developed in Articles 49 and 50 of the preliminary draft text (CONVENT 45)[1].

There is, of course, a certain re-assurance for anyone - whatever their thoughts on the nature of the Charter - on these Articles which seek to place the whole Charter with the context of Community competences. Though for the rabid anti-European Union scaremongers the very existence of such reassurances provides the opportunity to raise unfounded fears about a back door European Union take-over of all aspects of Member State law and competences.

Over the last eight months, I have been struck at how much of the occasional reporting on the Charter in the British press has tended to portray the Charter as a nascent European constitution under which governments will lose their powers and citizens their democratic rights and historic freedoms. This argument has then been supported with quotes from the minorities to be found at each end of the Euro-spectrum: a 'Federalist', who expresses the hope that this Charter will lead the way quickly to such a Euro constitution, and a 'Nation Statist', who vows to fight to the end against this perceived threat.

There is also the implication that all this is happening in dark corners in Brussels where members of the British media have to use every sort of investigative subterfuge to bring the whole Charter process into the light of day. The truth is, of course, that all of the Convention's proceedings are held in public and that all of the Convention documentation in the on-going Charter process can be drawn down from the Charter web site.

I strongly believe that the outcome of the Convention should be a Charter emphasising the legal protection and democratic rights of individual Union citizens and residents, the responsibilities of Union institutions and bodies and Member State governments to uphold the law and provide good administration, and the responsibilities of individuals in their own lives to uphold the ethos of the Charter in their respect for the dignity of other people, human rights, democracy and the rule of law. The critical debate should not be about getting hung up on the wilder shores of the Charter as a nascent European Union constitution, but the realities of creating practical processes to give effect to the Charter in promoting these individual and institutional rights and responsibilities in the context of the European Union.

One area of critical concern is the way in which the ECHR will fit into the Charter, and a consistency be maintained in judgements made by the European Court of Justice and the European Court of Human Rights on issues which are common to the new Charter of Fundamental Rights and the ECHR, with its half century of case-law, determining the levels of protection given. The Charter of Fundamental Rights must be clear on the role of the ECHR law in providing minimum levels of protection. It must also ensure that the obligations of the European Union's institutions and bodies are consistent with those of its Member States. For whilst the Member States of the European Union are signatories of the ECHR, the Commission is not. The Charter must make provision to deal with the potential inconsistencies that could arise with charges of a two-tier system of protection developing between Strasbourg and Luxembourg: between Council of Europe members in the European Union and those which are not.

The French government has led the argument against the need to refer to the ECHR case-law in the Charter whilst the British Government has been in the vanguard of these arguing for such a reference. The ideal solution would be to allow the

Commission to become a signatory to the ECHR but this, of course, has its own political and legal difficulties. The European Court of Justice ruled in 1994 that the Commission did not have the legal standing to sign up to the ECHR. On the political point it also raised issue about the potential 'Statehood' of the Commission and the Community assuming the same identity as a state.

I am confident that a way will be found to deal with this problem which has aroused considerable concern in the Council of Europe and the European Court of Human Rights.

I have found the debate within the Convention to be constructive and good-natured. The occasions have been few when tempers have been aroused and stand-offs threatened. This has been to the credit of its members and the Presidency in the Chair, particularly of President Herzog. Thus I remain optimistic that the movement which will be needed to complete successfully the Charter process will be achieved.

Notes

1 These are now Articles 51 and 52 in the final draft (COVENT 50).

Chapter 5

Contribution to the Federal Trust publication on the EU Charter of Fundamental Rights

Lord Russell-Johnston

Writing from a Council of Europe perspective, this chapter looks at the potential problems a legally binding Charter could cause in relation to the ECHR. It draws the scenario of two parallel supranational mechanisms for the protection of fundamental rights in Europe. It raises concerns about the ECJ becoming the last instance of appeal in the EU for human rights issues which might result in a downgrading and weakening of the ECtHR and deprive EU citizens of a final external appeal against alleged violations of their fundamental rights. The idea of an EU Charter, even a legally binding one, is not rejected. But to avoid competing jurisdictions and strengthen the protection of human rights in the EU it is concluded that the only logical way forward is for the EU to accede to the ECHR.

The remainder of the chapter summarises the official resolutions and reports of the Council of Europe Parliamentary Assembly on the matter.

A legally binding Charter that would not be followed by accession of the European Union to the European Convention on Human Rights would create two parallel jurisdictions, two competing supranational mechanisms to protect human rights. That is the basic problem.

'Is that necessarily bad?' you may say. After all, two parachutes are better than one.

Yes, as long as you do not try to open them both at the same time.

At the moment, 850 million Europeans, after having exhausted all remedies at the national level, have the possibility to take their grievances to the European Court of Human Rights in Strasbourg. 850 million from the Isle of Skye to Grozny. They may seek justice at the same place, and their complaints will be examined by the same body and according to the same rules. It is a bit of an administrative nightmare, but, at the same time, it is also a huge achievement - one court for one Europe. If the European Union proceeds with creating a parallel system for the protection of human rights, with the European Court of Justice in Luxembourg as the last instance of appeal, for the very same rights protected by the Human Rights Convention, creating a new source of potentially conflicting jurisprudence, I think this will inevitably weaken and undermine the broader mechanisms with the Strasbourg Court at its core.

With two competing mechanisms, the EU fifteen, or soon perhaps a few more, would logically be expected to favour the new Court, that is the Luxembourg Court, excluding the possibility of having potentially sensitive cases decided upon by judges from non-EU Member States.

For the countries not yet members of the EU, which are members of the Council of Europe, potential implications of a second human rights mechanism would be even more disturbing.

With the EU fifteen shifting to Luxembourg as their instance of final appeal, the Court of Human Rights would become the court for the 'rest of Europe', perceived by many as downgraded and weakened, with its authority and respect for its decisions inevitably undermined. What that would mean in cases such as the Court's order to stay the execution of Abdullah Ocallan, for instance, is not difficult to predict.

With regard to cases concerning violations allegedly committed by European Union institutions there would be another problem created, which has so far been largely ignored.

In this scenario, the court of final appeal - the Luxembourg Court - would be part of the same legal and political entity - the European Union (Community, for the purists) - as the institution that has allegedly committed the violation.

For all practical purposes, the Luxembourg Court is to the European Commission what the highest court is to a government at national level. With appeals stopping in Luxembourg, European Union citizens would lose the possibility of a final external appeal, which is the essence, and indeed the *raison d'être* for the European Convention on Human Rights and its enforcing mechanisms.

This is not a negligible problem, as it concerns a substantial and, with the expansion of European Union competence, a rapidly growing part of their rights protected by the Convention. Paradoxically, a major effort to strengthen the respect for human rights and fundamental freedoms could lead to the protection of these rights actually being weakened.

I want to make it quite clear that I am not against a European Charter, a legally binding one, provided, naturally, that it is followed by the accession of the European Union to the European Convention of Human Rights.

That, of course, creates other problems, which I am not going to go into, because they are largely legal. But my argument in favour of accession is rather simple. Fifteen European countries made a commitment to respect the European Convention on Human Rights, and agreed to submit themselves to the jurisdiction of the Strasbourg Court. They remained bound by this commitment even after they set up the European Union and in spite of the fact that they transferred some of their competence to Brussels. They are obliged to ensure that the Union is able to fulfil the obligations resulting from the Convention in exactly the same manner as they would have to fulfil them if the competence had not been transferred. Accession to the Convention is, logically, the only way to achieve that.

Seen in this light, the accession of the EU to the Convention is not a giant federal leap into the unknown, but an act dictated by the existing international obligations of the EU Member States.

The Convention drawing up the Charter has not yet concluded its work. There is still time to convince us that the main objective of the undertaking is to strengthen the protection of human rights within the European Union, and not merely to enhance the role of the European Union in protecting human rights.

Editorial Summary of the Council of Europe Parliamentary Assembly's views on the EU Charter

Based on a report by its Committee on Legal Affairs and Human Rights, the Parliamentary Assembly of the Council of Europe has adopted Resolution 1210 (2000) on the EU Charter of Fundamental Rights.

The Assembly welcomes the EU's initiative to adopt an EU Charter as a

> '[...] logical consequence of the evolution on both the European Institutions and in the Council of Europe towards the protection of human rights in Europe'.

However, it expresses concern that the protection of fundamental rights be coherent throughout Europe and that a solution be found that avoids two different sets of rights and two different categories of citizens.

It therefore emphasises the importance of the ECHR and recommends that the rights contained therein, and developed in the Protocols and the ECtHR's case-law should be included into the EU Charter so as to avoid the risk of weakening the ECHR. The Assembly points out that accession of the EU to the ECHR has long been an option favoured by the Council of Europe as it

> '[...] would form an important bond between the European Communities and the member states of the Council of Europe in the specific field of human rights and fundamental freedoms, and would thus contribute to strengthening the principles of parliamentary democracy and the implementation of basic human rights.' (Resolution 745 of January 1981).

The Report does not, however, see accession of the EU to the ECHR and the adoption of an EU Charter as mutually exclusive exercises. In this case, the Convention would provide the minimum standard of protection with the Charter potentially including additional rights, particularly social and economic ones. For these, recourse should be taken to the European Social Charter.

The Assembly recognises that there are risks regarding differing interpretations but is confident that these can be resolved by clearly defining the respective competences. The report proposes some options: The Strasbourg Court should continue to be responsible for the interpretation of the ECHR and the Luxembourg Court for the other rights, in particular those allegedly violated by EU institutions. The Courts could have the right to request prejudicial requests for an opinion of the respective other or their jurisdictions could be repartitioned according to the right involved or the accused organ or state.

The Resolution therefore concludes that the EU should

'[...] incorporate the rights guaranteed in the European Convention on Human Rights and its protocols into the charter of fundamental rights and to do its utmost to safeguard the consistency of the protection of human rights in Europe and to avoid diverging interpretations of those rights;

[...] pronounce itself in favour of accession to the European Convention on Human Rights of the Council of Europe and to make the necessary amendments to the Community treaties;

[...] make sure that when referring to social rights the revised European Social Charter of the Council of Europe will be taken into account.'

Chapter 6

EU Charter of Fundamental Rights - A Local Government Perspective

Jeremy Smith

This chapter - written by the author in a personal capacity - assesses the Charter from a local government perspective. It argues that as a result of changes in law and policy – most recently by the incorporation of the ECHR by the Human Rights Act – local authorities are undergoing a transformation from being largely administrative units created by central government to ensure more efficient provision of services to more integrated and generic entities entrusted with own rights, freedoms and obligations to guarantee and enforce citizens' rights. By promoting a more rights-based approach and culture in the EU, the Charter is perceived as working in synergy with these developments, replacing prevailing paternalistic attitudes of government at all levels. The Charter as well as its drafting process, however, meets with some criticism in particular as regards its unclear purpose and status which raise questions about its legal enforceability. There are also ambiguities about the content and application as some rights are included in the draft that clearly do not as yet fall into EU competence. It is argued that at this stage of the EU's development the Charter should – for the sake of clarity, simplicity and accessibility – have been drawn up as a mainly declaratory document not seeking to create new law or new means of enforcement.

Analysing the unknowable

Writing in late summer 2000, it is a tough task to assess the likely impact of the EU's Charter of Fundamental Rights on local government. Most of us may agree that, in some form, an EU Charter is an essential, or at least beneficial, step in the Union's evolution. As yet, however, we do not know the final contents - though, as I write, I have before me a consultation draft put out by the Charter 'Praesidium' - and, even more important, we have no idea of the likely status of the Charter. Even so, some key issues of principle have been raised which enable us to reflect on the possible contribution the Charter will make.

The timing of the Charter's finalisation adds to the uncertainty. Due to be adopted by the end of this year (whatever adopted may mean), the new Charter will appear just as local government, amongst others, starts to grapple with its new duties under the Human Rights Act 1998, in effect incorporating the European Convention on Human Rights into UK law.

UK local government - a new focus on rights?

For local government, the Human Rights Act has two facets. First, there is a need to ensure compliance with at least the letter, and preferably the spirit, of the Convention. Second, and longer term, it offers a new perspective, under which democratic local government embraces a new rights-based culture - and thus a new compact between local government and its citizens.

This requires a brief digression into the origins of British local government, which differs from most of our continental counterparts. Here, local government in its modern form came into being in the second half of the 19th century, as part of the utilitarian philosophy related to the Poor Law and the problems of public health in the cities. Local authorities (at first, for specific rather than general purposes) were set up by central government within boundaries it considered appropriate for dealing efficiently with the issues. Though functions and boundaries have changed radically over the years, central government has seen local government as its own creation, to be reformed and restructured according to central government's views on efficiency and effectiveness. The philosophy of *'ultra vires'*, under which local authorities can only do what statute permits, flows from this premise. In legal theory, local authorities have been assigned a set of individual services, evidenced in the service-specific language of 'local education authorities' or 'housing authorities', even though they form part of the single legal entity of the council.

It is only in this year's Local Government Act that a new power to promote the economic, social and environmental well-being of a local authority's area has been enacted, requiring in law a more integrated approach which focuses on the overall area and its citizens, not just the individual public service. Combined with the rights-based approach of the Human Rights Act, both central and local government will need to rethink their conceptual models of local government's role and rationale. The Greater London Authority, though not a local authority as such, is even more clearly tasked to look at the well-being of London as a whole, rather than as provider of a catalogue of individual services.

On much of mainland Europe, the history and emphasis has been quite different, even if the impact of industrialisation (and later, de-industrialisation) has led to many common issues along the way. The commune is mainly based on historic identity, not on utilitarian notions of administrative efficiency. In countries such as Germany and Italy, which only lately became nation states, the towns and cities have a long history of freedoms and rights that date back to medieval charters. Less encumbered by the restrictive tenets of *ultra vires*, there has been more space for locally determined action, and a stronger emphasis on rights. The Council of Europe's Charter of Local Self-Government reflects this approach. For all its caveats (many introduced by UK government lawyers!) this Charter reads in places more like a charter of municipal rights than a citizens' charter of rights to be delivered via local authorities.

Therefore, the new EU Charter of Fundamental Rights will be launched at a time when local government's role is slowly being redefined, and when a further shift from benevolent paternalism to a citizens' rights-based ethos is working its way through.

A debate that is yet to be had

At present, consciousness of the new EU Charter process is, in truth, minuscule within British local government. There are so many changes and duties to deal with under the government's 'modernisation' rubric, including now the Human Rights Act, that few have spared a thought for a new Charter of Rights with unknown content and unknown status.

Where discussion has taken place, amongst the UK delegation to the EU Committee of the Regions, and in the LGA's European and International Executive, the debate has focused more on party political positions on the EU than on any deeper analysis - which is not surprising, given the curious process adopted for drawing up the Charter, in particular the lack of clarity as to its purpose and ultimate status.

Thus, the Conservative members have tended not to see the need for an EU Charter at all, but if it is to exist, it should be declaratory only. The Liberal Democrat view has been to favour an EU Charter, and to favour at least some of it being legally enforceable. As for the Labour Party, there is a split between those who favour a wide-ranging, legally enforceable charter (and like the Liberal Democrats, seeing this as a major step towards a European constitution) and those who take the UK government's line of support for a declaratory charter, to make European citizens' rights more visible, but who profess to fear the 'lawyers' paradise' that another legally enforceable charter might bring.

So my starting point is based on first, a general lack of specific awareness or interest, and second, a lack of any common basis or agreement amongst those who have yet considered the general issues. In the absence of a policy 'line' from British local government, this article can only be a personal reflection on the important issues involved. I look first at the development of a rights-based European 'culture', second at the development of the Treaty of Rome's purposes and the European Union's objectives, and third at how the draft Charter - process and content - relate to these.

A European rights-based culture

The history of 'human rights' is often seen as a product of the late 18th century, with the American Bill of Rights and the French Declaration des droits de l'Homme - both products of revolutionary processes. There is, of course, an English line of earlier development, from Magna Carta (at least as a retrospective contribution), the Petition of Right of 1628 (as part of Parliament's attempt to limit the royal prerogative) and the Bill of Rights of 1689. As befits the pragmatic English tradition, these texts dealt with current grievances rather than matters of political philosophy, and developed the British tradition of protecting rights through procedural means (e.g. the writ of habeas corpus), which has later been an important tributary to the wider river of rights.

But it was, of course, the experience of two World Wars, fought heavily on European soil, that led to a stronger process of development of a culture of human rights in the second half of the 20th century. Therefore, the political drive that led to the development of the European Common Market was the same, from a different perspective, as that which led to the development of legally enforceable human rights - namely, the need to prevent future warfare in Europe.

In 1948, the General Assembly of the United Nations adopted the Universal Declaration of Human Rights, recognising (in the words of its Preamble) that

'[...] the inherent dignity and [...] the equal and inalienable rights of all members of the human family is the foundation of freedom, justice and peace in the world', and that 'disregard and contempt for human rights have resulted in barbarous acts which have outraged the conscience of mankind'.

The Declaration has never been directly legally binding, though it has had enormous influence in shaping subsequent human rights charters and law. It describes itself as 'a common standard of achievement for all peoples and all nations.' It sets out all of the 'classical' civil and political rights, but also includes a number of what have since been called economic and social rights, e.g. the right to social security, and the right to a standard of living adequate for the health and well-being of the individual and family, including food, clothing, housing and medical care and necessary social services.

The Universal Declaration is therefore a strong precedent for a form of 'charter' that has no direct legal effect, which is innovative in the range of rights it covers, and which nonetheless has a strong impact on public opinion and on future, more binding, human rights instruments.

This influence is expressly referred to in the Council of Europe's European Convention on Human Rights. Its Preamble includes the following:

'Being resolved, as the Governments of European countries which are like-minded and have a common heritage of political traditions, ideals, freedom and the rule of law to take the first steps for the collective enforcement of certain of the Rights stated in the Universal Declaration'.

The European Convention has been called

> 'the first essay in giving specific legal content to human rights in an international agreement, and combining this with the establishment of machinery for supervision and enforcement. However it is important to understand that [the role of the enforcement bodies] is that of review, and not that of an appeal court from the decisions of national tribunals. Their task is to ensure that the standards of the Convention [...] are observed by the administrations of the States concerned.' (Professor Ian Brownlie).

Moreover, the Preamble also shows that it was seen as the first, not as the final, step in the collective enforcement of the rights set out in the Universal Declaration, and the subsequent Protocols to the Convention have indeed developed the content of rights further.

Events in Central and Eastern Europe since 1989 have led to a doubling of the membership of the Council of Europe, with today over 40 states belonging. Adhesion to the European Convention has been an essential requisite of the membership process - which means that citizens from Vladivostok to Lisbon have the right of access to the Court of Human Rights in Strasbourg.

So the European Convention has expanded from being a means of cementing the states of Western Europe in a common ethos of human rights, to providing a unifying philosophy of rights - at least on paper - for the whole of 'wider Europe'.

The rights in the European Convention are mainly the classical civil and political rights, not the economic and social rights. Moreover, the original text excludes the provisions of the Universal Declaration on democracy, whose Article 21 provides:

> '1. Everyone has the right to take part in the government of his country, directly or through freely chosen representatives.
>
> 2. Everyone has the right of equal access to public service in his country.

3. The will of the people shall be the basis of authority of government; this will shall be expressed in periodic and genuine elections which shall be by universal and equal suffrage and shall be held by secret vote or by equivalent free voting procedures.'

These rights only appear in the First Protocol, in a form which reduces the 'will of the people' to the 'opinion of the people', whose Article 3 provides:

'The High Contracting Parties undertake to hold free elections at reasonable intervals by secret ballot, under conditions which will ensure the free expression of the opinion of the people in the choice of the legislature.'

(The draft EU Charter, it may be noted, whilst stating in the Preamble that it is based on the principle of democracy and the rule of law, sets out no version at all of the right to democracy, whilst, however, providing for the right to stand and vote at European and municipal elections.)

The economic and social rights, which the European Convention does not cover, are set out in another Council of Europe charter, the 1961 European Social Charter. This Charter has a system of monitoring and review, but no direct legal enforcement. This difference is reflected in the wording of Part I:

'The Contracting Parties accept as the aim of their policy, to be pursued by all appropriate means, both national and international in character, the attainment of conditions in which the following rights and principles may be effectively realised [...].'

An 'aim of policy' to attain conditions in which rights and principles may be realised is a long way from direct legal enforcement by any individual citizen. It reflects the fact that most of the economic and social rights have major potential economic consequences, that many of them have been achieved through collective bargaining and other non-statutory means - and that states would not welcome handing over broad policy decisions to an international tribunal of judges.

66

The development of the objectives of the Treaty of Rome and the European Union

The Treaty of Rome of 1957 was, of course, an economic treaty - it set up a common market, and its objectives reflected this. The Preamble referred to 'economic and social progress' and affirmed

'[...] as the essential objective of their efforts the constant improvement of the living and working conditions of their peoples'.

The signatories 'resolved by thus pooling their resources to preserve and strengthen peace and liberty'. Article 2 set out the Community's task as being

'[...] to promote throughout the Community a harmonious development of economic activities, a continuous and balanced expansion, an increase in stability, an accelerated raising of the standard of living, and closer relations between the States belonging to it.'

The Preamble to the Single European Act (SEA) of 1986 included the first Treaty references to human rights:

'Determined to work together to promote democracy on the basis of the fundamental rights recognised in the constitutions and laws of the Member States, in the Convention for the Protection of Human Rights and Fundamental Freedoms and the European Social Charter, notably freedom, equality and social justice [...]

Aware of the responsibility incumbent upon Europe to aim at speaking ever increasingly with one voice [...] in particular to display the principles of democracy and compliance with the law and with human rights to which they are attached [...].'

The actual content of the SEA, as it amended the Treaty of Rome, did not bear specifically on human rights issues, however, and the main changes to the Treaty (internal market, economic and monetary policy co-operation, cohesion, environment) did not touch on rights issues.

The Treaty on European Union (Maastricht) of 1992 is the first to contain substantive references to human rights. The Preamble more clearly confirmed the Member States'

'[...] attachment to the principles of liberty, democracy and respect for human rights and fundamental freedoms and the rule of law.'

The new European Union Treaty (as distinct from the European Community Treaty) included Article F:

'1. The Union shall respect the national identities of its Member States, whose systems of government are founded on the principles of democracy.

2. The Union shall respect fundamental rights, as guaranteed by the European Convention for the Protection of Human Rights and Fundamental Freedoms [...] and as they result from the constitutional traditions common to the Member States, as general principles of Community law.'

The Maastricht Treaty also introduced the concept of European Union citizenship, though with a limited raft of rights (movement and residence, vote and stand as candidate in European Parliament and municipal elections, consular protection, petition the Parliament and apply to the Ombudsman). Beyond this, however, there is nothing specific in terms of the Community's 'task' or activities that relates to human rights.

The most recent Treaty, that of Amsterdam in 1997, added a new Preambular head, which (following the Maastricht preamble's reference to human rights), confirms the Member States'

'[...] attachment to fundamental social rights as defined in the European Social Charter [1961] and in the 1989 Community Charter of the Fundamental Social Rights of Workers.'

Article 6 of Amsterdam subtly revises the wording of Article F of Maastricht, set out above. Whilst paragraph 2 (requiring the Union to respect fundamental rights etc.) is unchanged, a new paragraph 1 has been inserted:

'The Union is *founded* on the principles of liberty, democracy, respect for human rights and fundamental freedoms, and the rule of law, principles which are common to the Member States.' (My emphasis).

The reference to respecting the national identities of Member States is now a separate paragraph 3.

This reference to the Union being *founded* on principles of human rights, etc. is all the more important, since a new Article 7 enables the Council to determine the existence of a serious and persistent breach of the principles mentioned in Article 6(1), and to suspend the rights in the Council of a guilty Member State. This provision - given more focus by the recent case of Austria - adds weight to the case for defining these principles more clearly.

The EU Charter process

While the call for the EU to have its 'own' Charter of Rights is not new, it has only received official blessing since, and at, the German Presidency's Cologne European Council in June 1999. This is indeed logical, since it is only since Amsterdam was ratified that we have had an EU expressly founded on human rights.

The membership of the drafting body (later calling itself the 'Convention') was set out in outline, representing an innovative mix of governmental, parliamentary and Commission representatives.

The drafting body should produce a draft text by December 2000, following which

'[t]he European Council will propose to the European Parliament and the Commission that, together with the Council they should solemnly proclaim on the basis of the draft document a European Charter of Fundamental Rights.'

So far, so good. But then,

> 'It will then have to be considered whether and, if so, how the charter should be integrated into the treaties.'

This last point is bizarre. Treaties are legal documents, with legal effect. Charters may be legal documents, or declaratory documents. Until this point, the language is all about making rights more evident or more visible. But suddenly, a huge unknown, a giant uncertainty was thrown into the process.

As we know, the UK government has only wanted a 'declaratory' Charter, one that makes rights more 'visible'. Opponents of this view pour scorn on such a weak Charter, though the UN Declaration shows that not all such texts need be weak in their impact.

Immediately, the issue changed from being one about human rights in the context of the European Union, to being one about the future shape of Europe's governance. Those wanting a European constitution have seen the Charter as a way of making progress - and the more integrated into the Treaties, the better. Those opposed to further European integration have seen the whole initiative in politico-constitutional terms also, and have tended to be cautious about the whole idea of a Charter.

The framework of the summer 2000 draft of the Charter of Rights is an interesting one, in that it seeks to escape from the 'old' labels of civil, political, economic and social rights. Rather, its chapters are headed Dignity, Freedoms, Equality, Solidarity, Citizenship and Justice. This has the merit of putting all the rights of EU citizenship (not, as yet, a long list) into a single chapter, which may be important when it comes to enforceability. We may also understand that the drafting 'Convention' has tackled its task on the basis that, since the Charter may later have legal effect, it should be drafted with this in mind. If so, then its generally terse and understandable language (a big plus in terms of wider citizen understanding), and its lack of many explicit restrictions or qualifications, mean that it could be a source of plentiful litigation in future, in whatever legal arena may apply.

There is still, however, a central ambiguity or contradiction. Is it a text of the rights of citizens within the EU's Member States, whether or not the subject matter is within the EU's competences, or is it a Charter of Rights that applies only to the EU as such?

The Preamble asserts that '[e]ach person is therefore guaranteed the rights and freedoms set out hereafter.'

But through what means is the guarantee to be delivered? If, as draft Article 49 (now 51) provides, the provisions of the Charter are addressed to the EU and the Member States when implementing EU law, and if no new powers are granted to the Union, then the issue of future legal enforcement is already constrained - and the citizen will not be able to look to the European Court of Justice to meet the 'guarantee' of his or her rights, save in limited circumstances related to European citizenship, or acts by the EC or EU, within its existing powers, that contravenes any of the Charter's provisions. There will, of course, be such cases.

But that is a far cry from a legally enforceable Charter akin to the European Convention. The Charter says, after asserting the general 'right to life', that 'no one shall be condemned to the death penalty, or executed' (draft Article 2). The EU has, within its mandate, some quite tough powers of enforcement, but these do not extend to the death penalty for non-compliance with EC Directives. So this provision of the Charter will have no bite as far as the EU is concerned. This Article is, of course, a right addressed to the Member States (present and future), and is similar to the provisions of a Protocol to the European Convention outlawing the death penalty. The only foreseeable impact of this Article on the EU, as it stands, is in relation to Article 7 TEU, under which a state can be suspended for serious and persistent breaches of human rights.

To take another example, the rights to marry and found a family are set out in draft Article 9, 'in accordance with the national laws governing the exercise of these rights'. Whilst the EU might do something that affects these rights, they are, of course, of far wider import, and are in essence covered by the European Convention (which also refers to national laws). The citizen claiming a breach of these rights can therefore use the courts of the Member State in question, and can apply to the European Court of Human Rights under the European Convention if the Member State acts in breach of the right.

Draft Article 50(3) (now 52(3)) provides that, insofar as the new EU Charter contains rights that 'correspond to' European Convention rights, the meaning and scope of those rights shall be similar, 'unless this Charter affords greater or more extensive protection.' This will open up some difficult questions in future of whether rights do correspond, what 'similar' means, and so on.

A wider set of uncertainties is provided in draft Article 50(1) (now 52(1)), which provides that any limitation on the rights recognised by the Charter must be provided for by the competent legislative authority, subject to the principle of proportionality.

But who decides on the necessity, or otherwise, of these limitations? If the Charter has some effect by being incorporated into the EU Treaties, then the ECJ will presumably decide these questions, insofar as the alleged breach of the right relates to EU competences. If it does not, then the ECJ will not be able to deal with it in any event. If the Charter is not legally enforceable at all, then there is no court that will decide what the scope of necessary limitations may be.

Conclusion

I have concentrated above on some of the difficulties that I foresee in giving effect to the new EU Charter. However, the EU is at the right stage - especially on the eve of enlargement - to provide itself with a form of Charter that defines human rights. It needs this both to demonstrate that it is indeed founded on human rights values, but also to ensure that it has a clear statement that can be relied on, in case any Member State seriously and persistently breaches human rights standards.

At the same time, I believe that the process used has been flawed. The form the 'Convention' has taken may please those who follow EU affairs closely. But the lack of clarity of purpose, and the lack of clarity about the eventual status of the Charter, means that no sensible, comprehensible public discourse can take place. Even now, with an actual text to work from, it is impossible to tell what its consequences will be.

I can, of course, identify many draft Articles which touch upon local government business. As stated at the outset of this article, the Human Rights Act means that local authorities in the UK are having to sensitise themselves to the nature, and hopefully the culture, of rights set out in the European Convention. These include 'due process' rights, in the many cases where local authorities act in a quasi-judicial capacity. The draft EU Charter will add new rights that affect local government, for example protection of personal data, integration of persons with disabilities, the right of children to protection and care and to express their views freely. Some of the new 'solidarity' rights affect local authorities as large-scale employers (e.g. the right of access to placement services, and the right to reconcile family and professional lives). To take another example, Article 32(3) (now 34(3)) provides for rights in relation to social assistance and housing.

Housing benefit is very much a local government 'business', and the recognition of its importance in the social protection system is welcome - but what does this Article mean, given that housing benefit and social assistance generally are not Community tasks? How can this right be guaranteed?

I believe that, at this stage, the EU should have drawn up a Charter which did not seek to create new law, or new means of enforcement. The Charter could include creative new elements, and its coverage of rights might have been very similar to the current draft. As with the UN Declaration of Human Rights, this mainly declaratory Charter would be a basis to extend legal protection and enforceability in the future. It would be a key standard-setting text for the future, rippling out far beyond the EU's boundaries. The European Convention itself could be amended in the light of the new EU Charter, to pick up some new rights, or new formulations of old rights.

One key right missing in the current draft is the right to democracy, even though democracy and the rule of law are asserted as founding principles. The right to local self-government (provided for in the European Charter of Local Self-Government) is also lacking. These are important omissions which I hope the final text will put right.

I refer to a *mainly* declaratory EU Charter, because the signing of such a Charter would provide a definition of fundamental rights on which to base the power of the Council to suspend one of its members under Article 7 of the Treaty. Moreover, the ECJ would undoubtedly develop its jurisprudence to take the Charter's provisions into account.

I also envisage that the Charter would indicate, on its face, how citizens could seek redress for alleged breaches. For rights based on the European Convention, they would be 'sign-posted' to the Court of Human Rights, for many other rights, to the Member States, and for a few rights (related to EU citizenship) also to the European Court of Justice. Some rights would not have, at this stage, any means of direct enforcement.

There is one major lacuna in human rights coverage within

the EU, namely the fact that the EU and its institutions are not bound by the European Convention. The House of Lords Report on the Charter recommended that this gap be remedied by the EU 'signing up' to the Convention. This is certainly desirable, and would mean that any alleged breaches of the Convention by the EU could be taken to the Court of Human Rights. If this requires a Treaty amendment, so be it.

What we are seeking is a change in governmental culture, from a 'government knows best' attitude to one based on citizens' rights. This also applies to local government, long a bastion of paternalistic administrative culture. The Human Rights Act is a crucial step along the road of changing attitudes within all spheres of government in the UK. The EU institutions need also to be brought within a similar rights-based legal framework, in relation to their competences. But when it comes to legal effect and enforcement, let us keep it at least fairly simple, fairly clear. And let us ensure that the expansion of enforceable human rights, via the European Convention, now covering 41 countries, is continued.

Postscript

Since writing the above, the text of the draft Charter has been through two further drafts. The latest (CONVENT 50 from end September) affects a few points in the above article. In particular, the Preamble no longer states that

> '[e]ach person is therefore guaranteed the rights and freedoms set out hereafter.'

Rather, and very differently, the new text states that

> 'The European Union therefore recognises the rights and freedoms and principles set out hereafter.'

This means that the role of the Charter is becoming clearer - it is not a general guarantee of human rights, but a statement of rights recognised by the EU.

Another problem has been reduced by new wording, in relation to rights which 'correspond to' European Convention rights. New Article 51(3) - which was Article 50(3) when the Article was written - provides that the 'meaning and scope of those rights shall be the same as those laid down' by the European Convention. The previous draft said the meaning and scope would be 'similar', leaving room for uncertainty. The new text also states that this provision 'shall not prevent Union law providing more extensive protection.'

The reference to housing benefit in the earlier text has been changed to 'housing assistance'.

Finally, the new text still has no reference to a right to democracy, let alone (as we would wish) a right to local democracy. The new preamble has changed the reference to the principle of democracy to the values of democracy.

This omission is interesting - is it a reflection of a wider democratic deficit, or some other philosophical problem with defining democracy as a right of citizens?

Chapter 7

(Un) Charted Waters: The Legal Background to Fundamental Rights Protection in the EU

Michael Meehan

This chapter outlines the legal background to the Charter. It tells the story of EU fundamental rights protection by depicting the efforts of various institutional actors to establish a rights discourse at EU level. It argues that the ECJ deserves most credit for responding to the increasing need to protect individuals against human rights violations by EC institutions. It took the initiative by introducing the notion of human rights as general principles of EC law whose application it was under a duty to ensure. These general principles were initially inspired by the common constitutional traditions of the Member States and later put on a more coherent and consistent basis by reference to international human rights treaties (specifically the ECHR). This creative approach by the Court, born out of the lack of explicit legal basis in the original Treaties, is critically assessed as to its effectiveness for guaranteeing human rights, and it is argued that general principles take a subordinate place to - and can thus be restricted by - constitutionally protected rights, i.e. treaty-based EC objectives. The draft Charter is then critically assessed, and presented as a general move from political process to legal protection of individual human rights in the EU polity.

Introduction

The good ship European Union (EU), boldly going where no international or supranational legal institution has gone before in its ever-increasing scope and depth of competences, has provoked fears that its concern for the rights of its crew, those living within its borders, has taken a very definite second place to its concern to focus on more functional issues such as creating the conditions necessary for the operation of the Internal Market. Added to these concerns is the perception that by chipping away at the sacrosanct principle of national sovereignty, the growth and spread of European law and policies weaken the particular forms of rights protection developed over long periods at the national level. For the UK, Parliament's role as the ultimate guarantor and protector of liberties has been seen by some as having been usurped by the legal assault on parliamentary sovereignty represented by the principle of the primacy of Community law over inconsistent national law. For Germany, the Federal Constitution or 'Grundgesetz' is the ultimate source of reference for rights protection within German law and the German courts must give expression to this doctrine even where Community law challenges this. For judges of the higher Irish courts the legal prohibition of abortion is interpreted by reference to a provision of the Irish Constitution and not by reference to the Community freedom to provide services. As European integration has deepened, the criticisms and fears of the status of rights protection within the EU have increased, and the need for some clear response at the European level has become more acute. One such response has been the Cologne decision of June 1999 to draft the EU Charter of Fundamental Rights.

But what actually has been the real story of the protection of fundamental rights within the EU? This contribution will seek to highlight the main features of this story leading to the Cologne decision in June 1999 to draft the Charter. It will highlight the fundamental role of the European Court of Justice

(ECJ) in the development of the discourse of rights within the European Community. It will finally point out some of the challenges raised by the decision to draft such a Charter.

Navigating a course: Rights, treaties and institutions

The Treaties of the EU

Let us begin with a look at what is called the 'primary law' of the EU, the Treaties.[1] These constitute the Union's base and legal framework. The founding Treaties of the 1950s made no mention of a commitment to protect human rights at the Community level. Various explanations have been given for this, but they mainly focus on the fact that the building of the Communities was a functionalist process with a heavy emphasis on the creation of an economic space guided by liberal free market principles. On a national level rights were duly seen to be guaranteed or protected by parliaments or constitutional provisions, and instruments such as the European Convention on Human Rights (ECHR) obliged states to meet certain rights standards under international law.

The Single European Act of 1986 amending the 1957 Treaty of Rome introduced in its Preamble the first direct reference to the notion of protecting fundamental rights. The new Article F of the Maastricht Treaty on European Union (TEU) of 1992 took a more concrete step forward. It provided that:

> 'The Union shall respect fundamental rights as guaranteed by the ECHR [...] and as they result from the constitutional traditions common to the member states as general principles of Community law.'

This amendment recognised the particular importance and place of the ECHR in the development of a rights discourse in the EU, and reflected the tried and tested formula that had been developed incrementally by the ECJ in its jurisprudence to which I will turn later. In introducing citizenship of the EU, the Treaty also created particular rights resulting from this status.

The 1997 Treaty of Amsterdam marked another step forward. A new provision was added to the old Article F above to form a new Article 6 TEU. It provides in its first section that:

'The Union is founded on the principles of liberty, democracy, respect for human rights and fundamental freedoms, and the rule of law, principles which are common to the Member States.'

The possibility of suspending a Member State's voting rights within the Council for 'serious and persistent' breaches of the above principles is made possible under Article 7. Most importantly, the Court of Justice is given a wider jurisdiction to supervise the actions of the institutions in the light of the principles contained in Article 6(2). Freedom of movement is enshrined in a policy to develop an area of freedom, security and justice, both under Title IV EC Treaty and under Title VI TEU. The legal basis for the development of a policy of non-discrimination, building on the former Article 119 prohibiting discrimination in pay between men and women at work, is laid down in a new Article 13 EC Treaty. The Commission is given the responsibility of preparing legislation to empower the victims of discrimination in the field of application of Community law.

The response of the institutions

Although it is sometimes presumed by Europhiles that the EU and the former communities have long had a significant role in the promotion of human rights, the official story tells a different tale. It is generally accepted that the political institutions of the Union followed the lead of the Luxembourg Court in developing the notion of rights protection in relation to acts of the Community. The first real specific reference by them to human rights is contained in the Joint Declaration on Fundamental Rights of the European Parliament, Council and

Commission of 1977. The institutions stressed 'the prime importance they attach to the protection of fundamental rights', derived from the two sources of the constitutions of the Member States and the ECHR. The latter represented a common source of commitment to respect of human rights for the nine Member States at the time.

The Commission has, since the mid-70s, gradually played a more significant role in the process of developing a human rights discourse within the framework of European integration. After first rejecting the need for accession to the ECHR and expressing its support for the Luxembourg court's approach in a report in 1976, it later changed its view and advocated such a proposal in 1979. This did not meet with much favour, and other issues like the progressive moves towards increased economic integration came to dominate the business of Council and Commission during the 1980s. The Commission renewed its proposal for accession in 1990, and the path was paved to the famous *Opinion 2/94* of the ECJ in 1996 rejecting the possibility of accession by the European Community to the ECHR without a Treaty amendment, the creation of rules relating to fundamental rights being deemed by the Luxembourg Court not to be within the competences of the Community.

The European Parliament has passed numerous declarations and resolutions relating to rights and has identified the promotion and protection of fundamental rights as one of its primary concerns as a representative assembly. The strongest example of this commitment is the 1989 Declaration of Fundamental Rights and Freedoms. This Declaration listed a series of rights that were also contained in the ECHR, as well as providing for rights already included in the Treaties, such as Article 141 providing for equal pay between men and women for equal work. An innovative aspect was the inclusion of principles of democracy and of consumer protection and respect for the environment.

The Council's role in the promotion of human rights issues has been an important one as it brings together members of the governments of the Member States in its decisions and declarations. However, it has been more concerned with human rights as an aspect of foreign policy rather than focusing on the question of the quality of rights protection within the EU. The 1999 Cologne decision is the first serious attempt to realign its emphasis.

However, the most important actor in the development of the protection of fundamental rights in the EU has been the European Court of Justice. In many ways the story of the development and recognition of the importance of fundamental rights protection within the European Union has been a voyage of discovery pioneered by the ECJ, a course navigated by reference to international human rights standards (and in particular the ECHR) and to national constitutional standards of rights protection. In this sense rights protection within the EU has followed a charted course navigated by the jurisprudence of the ECJ.

Setting course: The ECJ and rights as 'general principles of Community law'

The development of the doctrines of supremacy and direct effect by the ECJ, coupled with the ever-increasing scope of Community law led to fears that the potential for human rights violations by the Community institutions or Member States implementing Community law was increasing.

The Luxembourg Court took the initiative over other institutions in opening the potential for a rights discourse in the Community order in response to arguments presented by applicants in litigation. Building its own judicial precedent over time, it was to award an increasing prominence to the ECHR. The first cases that can be highlighted which illustrate a preliminary reluctance on the part of the ECJ in recognising the value of fundamental rights in Community law are those of *Stork* and *Geitling*.[2] Both cases were challenges to decisions of the executive body (the High Authority) of the European Coal and Steel Community, taken in order to prevent the development of cartels in the coal industry. Both cases involved claims that the Basic Law ('Grundgesetz') of the German constitutional order should have been taken into account in the examination of the legality of the High Authority's decisions. The ECJ refused to entertain such a possibility. These decisions have been interpreted by some as logical in that they recognised the mainly functional and economic character of Community law at the time, and by others as indicating the concern of the Court to set the parameters of its own legal competence, fundamental rights not being a part of this competence.

In its desire to consolidate the uniformity of Community law within the Member State legal orders, the principle of supremacy was developed in a series of well-known cases leading from the decision in 1964 in *Costa v ENEL*.[3] The problem now was that a legal void had been created where national courts were not permitted to overrule Community law and the Luxembourg Court could not apply national law (including constitutional provisions relating to human rights) in its deliberations. The end result was that no clear protection was afforded to human rights in the supervision of Community law by the ECJ.

The Luxembourg Court took the initiative in reacting to this by introducing the notion of human rights being a part of the general principles of Community law whose application it was the Court's duty to ensure. In the case of *Stauder*, the Court made its first reference to fundamental rights.[4] The applicant objected to having to disclose his name to benefit from a particular social welfare scheme, claiming it violated his rights under the German Constitution. The ECJ held that the fact that Mr Stauder had to provide his name according to a particular interpretation of the legislation regulating the scheme was not

'[...] capable of prejudicing the fundamental rights enshrined in the general principles of Community law and protected by the Court.'

This meant that such provisions could not be interpreted in a way so as to violate an individual's fundamental rights as they formed part of EC law.

Human rights finally had a place in the legal discourse of the ECJ, located in general principles of Community law. The difficulty now was how to develop this protection in a logical and coherent fashion. This flexible source of 'general principles' created its own difficulties. The landmark supremacy case of *Internationale Handelsgesellschaft* pitted the German constitutional order against the ECJ over the issue of protection of fundamental rights.[5] After excluding the jurisdiction of the German Federal Constitutional Court to ultimately decide on the validity of Community law in relation to its own 'Grundgesetz' (Basic Law), the ECJ attempted to reassure the German Court that:

'In fact, respect for fundamental rights forms an integral part of the general principles of Community law protected by the Court of Justice. The protection of such rights, whilst inspired by the constitutional traditions common to the member states, must be ensured within the framework of the structure and objectives of the Community.'

When the case was referred to the German Federal Constitutional Court in what became known as the 'Solange' ('so long as') case[6], the Court set a series of conditions that had to operate in order for its own jurisdiction to safeguard fundamental rights to be replaced. They were that the law-making bodies of the Community had to be accountable to a democratically elected Parliament, and that rights protection had to be based upon a codified catalogue of rights.

This judicial shot over the bows of the ECJ led it to seek a certain source of legal stability for the future development of its rights jurisprudence. The European judges had indicated in the *Internationale Handelgesellschaft* case that fundamental rights as general principles are 'inspired' by the constitutional traditions of Member States. This source, however, was problematic. Even with the six countries at the time of the decision in 1970, the constitutional traditions were very different. Although it can undoubtedly be said that these countries shared certain common values, their expression in the various legal orders could be quite different.[7] This made it very problematic to clearly define individual rights at the Community level.

Professor Joseph Weiler has pointed out the difficulties in affording a maximal or minimal protection to a right by basing it on a level of importance recognised in one particular constitutional order. He also recognised that beyond a particular set of 'core fundamental rights', the protection of rights at the European level meets what he calls 'fundamental boundaries', where

'[...] in certain areas communities (rather than individuals) should be free to make their own social choices without interference from above.'[8]

Within the legal orders of states a particular fundamental right may express the meeting point of competing rights claims (e.g. individual interests v. state interests), this point indicating a balance based on the values of the society in question. If this is then considered a 'constitutional tradition' of the state, its transposition onto the European level imposes an understanding of values that may be at odds with other states' arrangements.[9] How was the Court to proceed?

We can see the first steps in the *Nold* case.[10] The case involved a challenge by a coal wholesaler to a Commission decision which the company claimed infringed their rights to property and to freely pursue an economic activity. Paragraph 13 of the Court's decision is worth quoting in full:

> 'As the Court has already stated, fundamental rights form an integral part of the general principles of law, the observance of which it ensures.
>
> In safeguarding these rights, the Court is bound to draw inspiration from constitutional traditions common to the Member States, and it cannot therefore uphold measures that are incompatible with fundamental rights recognised and protected by the Constitutions of those States.
>
> Similarly, international treaties for the protection of human rights on which the Member States have collaborated or of which they are signatories, can supply guidelines which should be followed within the framework of Community law.'

A second source for developing the protection of human rights as general principles of Community law was thus identified. International human rights treaties presented the advantage of providing a more coherent and consistent point of reference for rights protection in that they represent a fixed internationally agreed standard. The obvious human rights instrument at a regional level that could act as a 'guideline' for the ECJ was the ECHR. The French ratification of the latter in 1974 meant that all nine member states had a common source of commitment to international human rights protection. It contains a series of rights considered to be of universal value that represent a minimum standard of protection below which signatory states are not allowed to permit their protection to fall. This overcomes the difficulty of having to choose one national standard of protection. In the above citation, we see the roots of the future formula for defining and recognising rights within the Community/Union used in the case-law of the ECJ and in the Treaty amendments or declarations of the European institutions discussed above. In subsequent decisions, the ECJ referred to and gave particular prominence to the ECHR as the international source of rights protection it seemed to have in mind in *Nold*.[11]

A rather thorough examination of the question of rights protection and the relation between the ECHR, common constitutional traditions and fundamental rights as general principles of Community law, is contained in the case of *Hauer*.[12] The applicant wished to plant vines on her land but was prevented from doing so by a Community Regulation whose purpose was to curtail surpluses and improve the quality of wine production in the region. She claimed the Regulation effectively violated her rights to trade and to property as provided for in the German Constitution. The Court refused to recognise an infringement of these rights by the egulation while recognising the fact that the rights did exist as principles of Community law. In relation to the right to property, the Luxembourg Court recalled its two main sources of reference for locating rights and then investigated the possibility of restrictions to the right to property under the First Protocol of the ECHR. Finding a possible restriction to the right permitted for reasons of 'general interest' in the language of the Protocol, the court then turned to examining the protection of the same right under three national constitutional provisions. As Weiler notes, the court avoided the danger of the 'minimalist-maximalist' trap referred to above by subtly changing the language of its reasoning from earlier in the ruling (and departing thus also from previous decisions) from rights reflecting 'common constitutional traditions', to rights recognised as being 'in accordance with the ideas common to the constitutions of the Member States.' This resolution of the ECHR v. Member State standards dilemma allowed the court to go beyond the minimal standards laid down in the ECHR to develop criteria based on its own interpretation of what were 'ideas' common to the Member States and also on what would constitute an EC form of 'general interest'. Several difficulties however arise with this approach.

Choppy Waters: Weaknesses of this approach

The ECJ seeks, as indicated, to identify and protect fundamental rights as 'general principles of Community law.' In many ways recourse to this method is understandable. The Community judges have sought to permit a rights discourse by situating it in the judicially created sphere of general principles as a response to the absence of specific references to human rights in the founding Treaties, and to the lack of political will on the part of the Member States and the institutions (excluding perhaps the European Parliament) to give the EC a clear basis for fundamental rights protection. This is complicated further by the strict standing rules provided for by Article 230 TEC. These require a legal or natural person to show that a Community act is of 'direct and individual concern' in order to institute proceedings before the Court. By relying on 'general principles' the judges have given themselves a certain flexibility as to what rights they can recognise as meriting judicial protection and how it will be done. They have cleverly avoided the inherent problems discussed above of being forced to select particular national constitutional forms of rights protection by using the notion of 'ideas common' to Member States. They have also attained a certain stability of reference in acknowledging the common standard fixed by the provisions of the ECHR and its Protocols. Indeed, it can be said that the Court has relied more and more on the ECHR as a base for its derived principles. A clear example of this is the Luxembourg judges' reference in the *Hoechst* case to the ECHR as being 'of particular significance' to the recognition of fundamental rights as an integral part of the general principles of law.[13]

However, it can be argued that the consistency and effectiveness of human rights protection at the European level has been compromised by the ECJ following, or having to follow, this path. The protection of human rights at both the national (usually in the form of constitutional provisions) and the international level (in the form of human rights treaties) does not usually take the form of 'general principles.' The latter are usually legal ideas or values that supplement or enrich clear legal provisions. Under national constitutional law, fundamental rights as they may be protected usually take the form of clear provisions of some superior status of law and, if restricted in any way, the restriction is clearly defined and justified. In the realm of human rights law, a state agrees to comply under international law to agreed standards of rights protection. This protection is re-enforced by the ratification of such standards into a state's own constitutional legal order. The concept of general principles is more familiar to administrative lawyers where they are found at a level lower than constitutional or legislative norms in the hierarchy of laws.

The argument that 'general principles' are subordinate to, or complement and clarify, clearly stipulated constitutional provisions can also apply to the situation where a fundamental right recognised as a general principle by the ECJ has been made subject to a Community objective or interest. In many situations where the question of the existence of a fundamental right has been argued before, and recognised by the ECJ, a Community objective with a clear basis in the Treaties has been seen to be consistent with, or sometimes prevailing over the rights claim. In most of the cases examined by the Community judges the rights claimed have been recognised as valid ones by the Luxembourg Court, but the situations where an illegal violation was found have been few and far between.[14] The Court is open to accusations of appearing to favour those rights that more clearly reflect the economic function of the Community, and are consistent with the furthering of Community objectives having a firm legal basis in the Treaties such as the completion of the Internal Market. These goals have a firm legal grounding in the Treaties, unlike the protection of fundamental rights. The recent preliminary reference case of *Karlsson* follows a familiar pattern used by the Court.[15] It concerned the effect on the principle of equality of an interpretation of a Council Regulation establishing an additional levy in the milk sector. The claimants alleged that in the absence of clear provisions in the Regulation relating to how to allocate milk quotas, the Swedish legislation regulating such situations breached fundamental rights including equal treatment and non-discrimination. In its examination of the issues the Court stated at recital 45:

> 'However, it is well-established in the case-law of the Court that restrictions may be imposed on the exercise of those [fundamental] rights, in particular in the context of a common organisation of a market, provided that those restrictions in fact correspond to objectives of general interest pursued by the Community and do not constitute, with regard to the aim pursued, disproportionate and unreasonable interference undermining the very substance of those rights.'

There is an important point to be noted here. It may very well be the case that the ECJ's interpretation that a particular right has not been violated or can be made subject to restrictions based on Community objectives would be upheld by a human rights jurisdiction like the Strasbourg Court. But by exercising its own rights review based on flexible principles, and by not having its decisions made subject to the review of a human rights jurisdiction, the ECJ is open to criticism of favouring Community interests over individual rights. It can be argued that the idea of rights as general principles is simply not good enough (or legitimate enough) a substitute for EC/EU accession to the ECHR. Clearly formulated human rights norms are the bones of rights protection, general principles are at best the flesh that covers them.

Within national constitutional orders restrictions on the exercise or scope of fundamental rights exist. They are usually permitted in deference to ideas like the 'general interest', 'public order' or the like. However, by having constitutional value these very restrictions to rights are in a sense more democratically legitimate. Limitations are seen as necessary for a sort of 'greater good' based on a democratic notion of liberal constitutionalism. In each state a balance is found between the interests and rights of citizens and those of the organised expression of collectivity, the state. This balance is legitimated by its inclusion in the highest form of law. At the international level, and relative to our examination the ECHR, possible restrictions also exist. Thus, for example, for the ECHR there is the famous 'margin of appreciation' where signatory states are allowed a wide area of discretion to exercise restrictions to particular rights of the Convention. But the formula by which the Strasbourg Court will allow such restrictions is also founded on notions of liberal constitutionalism. They will only be permitted if 'necessary in a democratic society' seen in the light of particular criteria.

The ECJ may be many things, but it was not established as, and has not become, a Human Rights Court. According to Article 220 TEC, the Court is charged with the task of observing the law in the interpretation and application of that Treaty. Articles 2-4 of the EC Treaty provide the Court with the Community objectives and criteria to define the general interest of the Community. These objectives are mainly economic in character and do not always go hand in hand with liberal constitutionalist or human rights objectives, especially if the latter exist as imprecise and flexible principles.

The development of the Luxembourg Court's rights consciousness by its own method of general principles has opened the institution to various other criticisms. First, the Court is perceived as having expanded the influence of Community law into areas of great national sensitivity in developing fundamental rights as general principles of Community law. Second, the judges are seen as stepping on the toes of their Strasbourg counterparts who have clearly been given the role of protecting human rights throughout Europe under the aegis of the Council of Europe. So long as the two European jurisdictions remain separate from each other the potential for divergences in the jurisprudence of the two courts remains high.

The drafting of the Charter: Full steam ahead

The Vienna European Council of the EU formally issued a declaration affirming the 'primary importance' it attached to the UN Declaration of Human Rights on 10 December 1998.[16]

In it, it also emphasised its commitment to the notion of the universality and indivisibility of human rights and the Union's commitment to their protection, and it pledged its future support to their development. The publication of an annual Human Rights Report was called for and an interim report was submitted for consideration to the Cologne Summit in June 1999. In its concluding remarks, the document stated that it was 'an effort to make the EU's human rights policies more consistent and more transparent.' One of its effects was a European Council decision to establish a body to draw up an EU Charter of Fundamental Rights. The justification for such action reflected the language of the Report in that it was

'[...] in order to make their [fundamental rights] overriding importance and relevance more visible to the Union's citizens.'

The idea, it would appear, was to conduct a kind of compilation exercise of those rights already applicable at the Community/Union level, present them in an understandable and accessible form, and attempt to assuage claims that the EU as a polity lacked a coherent form of democratic legitimacy.

The European Council suggested that the body to draft this Charter should be made up of representatives from the various Union institutions as well as members of national parliaments with other institutions providing observers. A draft was requested ahead of the European Council Summit in Nice in December 2000. The Heads of State proposed that a solemn proclamation of a Charter of Fundamental Rights based on this draft be made by the Commission and Parliament. Whether and how the Charter would then become part of the Treaties framework would be considered after. The Tampere European Council in October 1999 established the rules concerning the composition, method of work and practical arrangements for the body to draft the Charter. It is composed of 62 members; 15 representatives of the Heads of State and Government of the Member States, one Commission representative, 16 designated members of the European Parliament, and two designates from each of the Member State parliaments. Two observers from the ECJ as well as from the Council of Europe were also selected. Particular bodies of the EU would be given hearings and 'other bodies, social groups and experts may be invited by the Body to give their views.'

Since its first meeting on 17 December 1999, the 'Convention', as it voted to call itself, has heard the views of many institutions, groups and individuals. All submissions and proposals have been reproduced on a web-site, giving a credible degree of openness to the whole process.[17] In September 2000 the Convention produced a final draft Charter of rights for presentation to the European Council meeting in Biarritz in October.

Unchartered waters: The challenges ahead

The draft Charter contains 52 articles, many of which are closely modelled on provisions of the ECHR. The rights contained stem from the ambit given in the Cologne decision, i.e. those rights recognised by the ECHR, rights of citizenship resulting from the changes made by the Maastricht Treaty, and economic and social rights insofar as they 'do not merely establish objectives for action by the Union.' The final form, scope and status of the Charter will be decided by the EU Heads of State in the final two summits of the French Presidency in October and December. However, by way of conclusion, serious challenges to the success of this project should be noted.

The question of the kind of rights to be contained in the Charter is a very problematic one and has been the source of much debate within and outside the Convention body. Familiar arguments relating to the justiciability of economic and social rights have been raised. The draft Charter proposes including a series of such rights under a general title of 'Equality'. This is a positive move for the concept of the universality of rights, and one hopes that their present inclusion will be accepted in the final form. There is a strong case for the inclusion of the rights contained in the European Social Charter as the social counterpart to those 'liberal' rights contained in the ECHR. Also, on the subject of the universality of rights, the draft Charter provides for the recognition of a diverse series of rights. However, is it truly possible to say that the right to have one's correspondence replied to in one of the official languages of the Union is of an equal status to the right to life?

The status, political or legally binding, to be given to the Charter is also a serious challenge. Having an EU Charter of Rights in the form of a political declaration may improve the 'visibility' of rights protected within the EU, one of the primary reasons put forward by the European Council for drafting the Charter. But if the Charter is not given a clear legally binding status it may suggest that concerns for image were more important than those of substance.

The relationship between the EU and the ECHR needs to be reassessed and the creation of a hierarchy of rights standards with different enforcement mechanisms and content would be a threat to both the consistency and effectiveness of rights protection within Europe. The issue of possible accession to the ECHR arises again and will need to be re-examined.

Is the Charter to cover all the legal framework of the EU and its institutions and bodies, or just the European Community? There are strong arguments for both extending the jurisdiction of the ECJ and the scope of the Charter to all of the EU.

Finally, the moves to draft a Charter represent a move in general from a political process of promoting and protecting rights through the use of political institutions to a legal protection of rights where judges, not the representatives of the people, ultimately decide on what our rights are. All these difficult challenges ahead make it clear that the EU polity is indeed entering uncharted waters.

Notes

[1] The European Coal and Steel Community, Euratom and the former EEC constitute the 'First Pillar', now called the European Community, of the 'European Union' created by the Treaty of Maastricht. The latter Treaty also created two other 'pillars', which, since the Treaty amendments brought about by the Amsterdam Treaty, are now called the 'Common Foreign and Security Policy' and 'Police and Judicial Co-operation in Criminal Matters' pillars.

[2] Case 1/58, *Stork v High Authority* [1959] ECR 17, and Joined cases 16 and 17/59, *Geitling v High Authority* [1959] ECR 17.

[3] Case 6/64, *Costa v ENEL* [1964] ECR 585.

[4] Case C-29/69, *Stauder v City of Ulm* [1969] ECR 419.

[5] Case 11/70, *Internationale Handelsgesellschaft mbH v Einfuhr- und Vorratsstelle für Getreide und Futtermittel* [1970] ECR 1125.

[6] *Internationale Handelsgesellschaft mbH v Einfuhr- und Vorratsstelle für Getreide und Futtermittel* [1974] 2CMLR 540.

[7] The right to property is a good example.

[8] Weiler, Joseph. 'Fundamental Rights and Fundamental Boundaries: On the Conflict of Standards and Values in the Protection of Human Rights in the European Legal Space.' in: *The Constitution of Europe.* Cambridge University Press, 1999. pp.103-104.

[9] The most graphic illustration of this dilemma was the competing rights claims in the Irish reference case of SPUC v Grogan. (Case C-159/90, *SPUC v Grogan* [1991] ECR I-4685).

[10] Case 4/73, *Nold v Commission* [1974] ECR 491.

[11] Some of the more important examples include: Convention rights that allow restrictions in Rutili; the right to a fair hearing in Cases 100-3/80, *Musique Diffusion Francaise v Commission* [1983] ECR 1825; the right to privacy and the extension of it to business premises by the ECJ in Case 136/79, *National Panasonic v Commission* [1980] ECR 2033 and Cases 46/87 and 227/88, *Hoechst v Commission* [1989]; Cases 97-9/87, *Dow Chemical Iberica v Commission* [1989] ECR 3165, non-retroactivity of penal provisions in R v Kirk; the right to a legal remedy in Case 222/84,

Johnston v Chief Constable of the RUC [1986] ECR 1651; freedom of expression in Case C-260/89, *ERT v DEP* [1991] ECR I-2925 and Case C-159/90, *SPUC v Grogan* [1991] ECR I-4685.

[12] Case 44/79, *Hauer v Rheinland-Pfalz [1979] ECR 3727.*

[13] *Hoechst v Commission (see n.11 above).*

[14] Many successful claims have involved rights of defence in competition and staff cases. For a comprehensive analysis of the ECJ's protection of fundamental rights see J.Weiler and N.Lockhart, 'Taking Rights Seriously: the European Court and its Fundamental Rights Jurisprudence' (two Parts), Common Market Law Review 32, pp.51-94 and 579-637.

[15] *Case 292/97, Karlssson, Judgement of 13/4/2000.*

[16] Declaration marking the 50th anniversary of the Universal Declaration on Human Rights.

[17] www.dbconsilium.eu.int

Chapter 8

The Proposed EU Charter of Fundamental Rights: Some Reflections on Its Effects in the Legal Systems of the EU and of Its Member States

Piet Eeckhout

This chapter concentrates on the Charter's legal status and its effects in the legal systems of the Member States – aspects considered of great importance for the direction the EU is moving into. It is argued that even if the Charter will not be incorporated into the Treaties by this IGC, it will eventually form part of the constitutional law of the EU. It will become a binding instrument complementing national and international human rights systems and providing greater legitimacy to the EU's - specifically the ECJ's - ongoing efforts to ensure effective protection of fundamental rights. It is further submitted that although the Charter is only intended to apply to the actions of EU institutions and Member States' authorities when implementing EU law, the specific status of EU law and its interconnectedness with national legal systems will cause legal difficulties and render it untenable to limit the Charter's scope in such a way - especially as the scope of EU legislative action expands. A binding Charter which takes fundamental rights seriously might well become a general vehicle for human rights protection in the Union.

Introduction

This short essay offers some initial reflections on the EU Charter of Fundamental Rights, particularly as to its legal effects.[1] The Charter gives rise to a host of interesting legal issues, which cannot all be examined within the scope of this contribution. After a general introduction, the discussion concentrates on two fundamental issues, namely the differences between making the Charter legally binding and adopting it as a mere political declaration, and the effects of the Charter in the legal systems of the EU's Member States. It is hoped that at the end of reading this essay the reader will be as convinced as the author that those aspects of the Charter, even though 'legal' and surrounded by technicalities, are of great import for the directions the European Union is moving into at the beginning of this century.

At the time of writing, which is in the last months of negotiation of the Charter, it is not yet decided what legal form (if any) the document will ultimately have. The negotiating forum, a fairly unique Convention, has been instructed not to address this issue. It is, however, obvious that the Convention is drafting the Charter as if it were a binding legal text. As it stands, the draft Charter could easily be incorporated in the EC Treaty or the EU Treaty. There are indications that the drafters are working on the assumption that, one day, that will indeed be the case. How else to explain, for example, that in several places the draft emphasises that some of the rights which it mentions do not confer any new competences or new tasks on the European Union? Such language is obviously of constitutional character, and is only required if the Charter were to form part of the founding Treaties. However, at this stage it seems highly unlikely that incorporation into the Treaties will take place on the occasion of the conclusion of the current IGC, scheduled for the end of this year. Such a decision would require unanimity among the 15 Member States, and some governments have already voiced opposition.

It is none the less interesting to examine what would be the legal effect of incorporation of the Charter in the founding Treaties.[2] The Charter would thus become highest law of the EU, of equal rank to all other provisions of the Treaties, and superior to EC legislation as well as to the laws of the Member States, the latter as a result of the established principle of the primacy of EC law. But does this mean that the Charter would with one stroke become the European human rights document *par excellence*? That, in order to find out which fundamental rights are vested in those living in the EU, one would automatically have to turn to the Charter? Such would clearly not be the effect of incorporation. The Charter is designed to be applied within the scope of European Union law only. It is primarily aimed at all forms of action by the EU institutions. It is not aimed at action by public authorities in the various Member States, other than where such public authorities are implementing European Union law.[3] As the European Union is ever-expanding its activities and law-making processes in all kinds of areas, it is considered desirable to ensure that, in the act, the protection of fundamental rights is fully ensured and safeguarded by having an express EU catalogue of fundamental rights against which EU action can be tested. However, the Charter is by no means designed to replace other forms of fundamental rights protection, such as those inherent in national constitutions or the geographically more broadly-based European Convention on Human Rights. The Charter should rather complement those systems by introducing a specific tool for human rights protection in the context of the EU.

Does this mean that, before there was the Charter, fundamental rights were not protected in the European Union? That it was - and is, as the Charter is not yet there in legally binding form - impossible for citizens in the European Union to contest action by the EU institutions as being in breach of fundamental rights? That is obviously not the current legal position.[4]

Fundamental rights are protected in the context of action by the EU's institutions, even though there is no fundamental rights catalogue in the current EU Treaties. The European Court of Justice established, already some decades ago, that fundamental rights are what it calls 'general principles' of EC law, and that, in the form of those general principles, they are binding on the EU institutions. The Court has itself constructed this notion of general principles, which was not present in the founding Treaties. But as the Court stands at the top of the EU's legal system, and has the authority ultimately to determine how EU law is to be interpreted and applied, the construction of fundamental rights protection by the Court is similar, if not identical, in its effect as would be express provision for protection in the Treaties themselves. Indeed, at the occasion of the negotiation of the Maastricht Treaty on European Union the Court's approach to fundamental rights protection was codified in what is now Article 6(2) of the TEU.

But it is one thing to proclaim that fundamental rights are to be protected; the next step is, of course, to determine which rights are to be considered fundamental, and to define them in provisions of law. It is obviously not the task of a court to draw up a catalogue of fundamental rights, and the Court of Justice has therefore chosen to determine which rights are protected in EU law by using a mechanism of reference: it seeks inspiration in international human rights instruments and in the constitutional traditions of the Member States. Again, this was confirmed by the drafters of the Treaties in Article 6(2) TEU.

All this means that, effectively, the European Union institutions are obliged to ensure that any legislation which they put on the books and any administrative or other action in which they engage do not violate certain standards of fundamental rights protection. The same goes for authorities of EU Member States, in those cases where they apply or implement EU law. In terms of remedies, the EU's general system of remedies applies. This means, for example, that any court or tribunal in a Member

State may, when faced with a case in which it is alleged that an EC legal act violates fundamental rights, refer the case to the European Court of Justice under the so-called preliminary rulings procedure (Art 234 TEC). The Court will then have to decide whether the act in question is lawful or unlawful, and if the latter, the act will be invalidated. Or, to take another example, citizens feeling aggrieved by an act of an EU institution may, under certain conditions (see Art 230 TEC), directly challenge such an act before the European Courts in Luxembourg (Court of First Instance and Court of Justice on appeal). As a conclusion it may be stated that, before there was a Charter, the EU had its own system of protection of fundamental rights. It was certainly not a perfect system, and some have heavily criticised the European Court of Justice for merely paying lip service to the idea of fundamental rights protection, but it is fair to say that the majority of commentators, academic and otherwise, regard the system as operating more or less satisfactorily.[5]

Binding or non-binding?

All this gives rise to two intriguing, if not fascinating, questions. The first is: if fundamental rights are already protected as described, why then is there any need for a new Charter? The second question is: what is the use of such a Charter if it is not made legally binding, but remains only a political declaration? It is not possible to examine and develop those questions in any depth within the scope of this contribution. The analysis here is limited to some comments on the second question, but those comments are also relevant for the first question.

On the face of things, it is indeed very peculiar for the EU to draft an elaborate Charter of Fundamental Rights, with provisions which are clearly negotiated and written with a view to be legally binding and enforceable, only to adopt it as a non-binding political declaration. It is, of course, in the very essence of fundamental rights that they *are* made binding.

There is a clear risk that adopting the Charter as a non-enforceable declaration will create great tension between aspirations and actual effect. It is clear that one of the strongest political currents which have led to this Charter is the political elite's striving to bring European integration closer to the citizens of Europe, to make Europe more tangible and relevant. There is no doubt that a lot of effort will be made to present the Charter as a major achievement in that respect, even by governments which are opposed to making the Charter binding.[6] But how can one reasonably make the case that the citizens of Europe will substantially benefit from a mere political declaration proclaiming their fundamental rights, without giving them the opportunity actually to enforce those rights? That frankly seems awfully patronising and may, in fact, be a recipe for further disenchantment with Europe. Perhaps there is some time for making the Charter binding, and it may not need to happen this year, at the occasion of the current IGC. And it is also arguable that EU citizens ought to have a say in the adoption of the Charter as a binding legal text, by way of referenda or otherwise. But it would seem like a very poor exercise in public relations if, in a few years' time, the Charter is still a non-binding political declaration with little or no practical effect.

As an academic working in the field of European law, I consider there to be great advantages to having a binding Charter of Fundamental Rights, incorporated in the founding Treaties. The Charter would provide much greater legitimacy to the efforts of the European Courts in Luxembourg towards ensuring effective protection of fundamental rights in the context of the workings of the European Union. The Charter would be a general road-map, whereas presently the Courts are having to find their way with the assistance of a mere compass, which is what the reference to rights protected in international instruments and in constitutional traditions amounts to. The Charter would also enrich and structure the language of fundamental rights protection employed by the

Courts, and it would put more of a spotlight on the rights dimension of the legislative and administrative action of the EU institutions. Some expert commentators have forcefully argued that the EU is generally in need of a human rights policy, and there is much to be said in support of that view.[7] Those commentators have also argued that such a human rights policy could be pursued on the basis of the existing Treaties, but that is, in my view, less persuasive. The EU institutions, their staff, and the representatives of Member States working in an EU context all take their cue from the Treaties. In that sense the rule of law is very strong in the EU. In the absence of a generally elected legislature and a government operating as the centre of policy-making and political discourse,[8] the legitimacy of EU public action is much dependent on the provisions of the founding Treaties, which provide the agenda for such action. A substantial EU human rights policy is therefore much more likely to come about when the Charter is incorporated into the Treaties.

However, as was mentioned in the introduction, the Charter is not likely to be incorporated into the Treaties at the occasion of the current IGC, and it would therefore seem that, for some years at least, the Charter will merely be a political declaration of some kind. Does this mean that the Charter will be devoid of legal effect for the foreseeable future? There are reasons to doubt that; in fact, to put it somewhat sharply, there are reasons to think that in terms of legal practice it does not matter very much, at least in some respects, whether the Charter is made binding or not. Such a statement, of course, calls for some further explanation.

As described above, the European Courts in Luxembourg already protect fundamental rights, which they characterise as general principles of EC law. It is already part and parcel of the everyday business of those Courts to hear and decide on human rights arguments in cases where the lawfulness of legislative or administrative action by the EU institutions is in issue. As was also mentioned, the European Courts in deciding such cases seek guidance in international human rights instruments and in the constitutional traditions of the Member States. In practice, the Courts increasingly rely on the European Convention on Human Rights, which has the advantage of being applicable in all the Member States and of laying down common minimum standards. Imagine what is likely to happen once the Charter is adopted, even if only as a political declaration. There can be little doubt that counsel for parties involved in litigation with a human rights dimension before the European Courts will try to find support for their case in the text of the Charter. They will not argue that the Charter applies as such, but they will refer to it in support of their argument. There will thus be pressure on the Courts to discuss the Charter. It is difficult to see the Courts resisting such pressure with a mere 'the Charter is not a binding legal instrument and therefore the Court has no jurisdiction to apply it'. Remember the legitimacy issue surrounding the protection of fundamental rights by the Courts, in particular as regards the determination and definition of which rights are to be protected, to what extent and how. The European Courts have had to struggle with all those issues without textual guidance - not of their own fault, of course, but because no such guidance was provided to them. However, once there is a Charter, the product of serious work by a Convention consisting of representatives of Member States, parliaments, and EU institutions, there is no lack of textual guidance any longer.

How then could the European Courts legitimately decide that the old approach of construing fundamental rights as cases come and go is to be continued *without* looking at and integrating the Charter in the process of fundamental rights protection? It seems to me that everything pleads in favour of such integration, but for the doctrinal legal argument that the Charter is not formally binding. My guess would be that the European Courts would easily overcome that obstacle, simply by using the Charter as confirmation rather than legal basis of their rulings on fundamental rights issues. And it is well known that courts are very able at playing with those notions; in other words, it is relatively easy for courts to characterise an element of law as mere confirmation of the Court's reasoning whereas that element was effectively the basis for the Court's decision.

One should add here that a large number of provisions of the Charter aim but to confirm and codify the European Courts' past approach to fundamental rights issues. It would therefore not be illogical for those Courts formally to acknowledge that that is the tenor of the Charter, and to give effect to its provisions in a manner which comes very close to how the Courts would apply them if the Charter were incorporated in the Treaties.

None the less, there are also provisions in the Charter which are more novel, at least in terms of the current position of EU law. For example, Article 21(1) of the Charter contains a general anti-discrimination clause which resembles Article 13 EC Treaty. The latter, however, does not itself purport to prohibit discrimination; it merely gives competence to the EC institutions to adopt legislation which prohibits the covered forms of discrimination. Article 21(1) of the Charter, by contrast, is a very general and unqualified prohibition of any discrimination based on a long list of grounds. It is difficult to see the European Courts giving full effect to such a prohibition as long as the Charter is not made legally binding (or, in this case, until there is EC legislation covering the prohibited forms of discrimination). This is but one example; there are other provisions in the Charter which do not appear to be based on the European Courts' existing case-law, for example, the Charter's chapter on Solidarity. One is therefore likely to see variation in the extent to which those Courts apply the Charter, depending on the type of provision parties seek to rely upon. This will be a delicate exercise for the European Courts, and the contentious cases are likely to be those in which reference is made to Charter provisions which are not an ostensible codification of the Courts' previous approach.

Effects on Member States

The EU is not (as yet) an instrument for the general approximation and integration of the protection of fundamental rights. Europe has another tool for building that wing of the common European house, namely the European Convention on Human Rights. Accordingly, the Charter is not designed to lay down norms of human rights protection which are to apply generally throughout the Member States of the EU, as was mentioned above. For the general public this may sound surprising, but it is emphatically the case that the Charter - whether made legally binding or not - does *not* purport to be of general application. The Charter has come about out of concern with fundamental rights protection in the context of action by the EU; it does not aim to address fundamental rights issues in the context of action by Member States of the EU which has no link with the activities of the EU itself. An example may clarify this. Suppose the Charter is incorporated in the EU's founding Treaties, and thus made legally binding. Further, suppose in a criminal trial in one of the Member States rights of defence issues are raised. If that trial is not in some way linked to EU action, the Charter will not apply, even though it provides for respect for the rights of defence in Article 48(2).

Does this mean that the Charter would only be binding on the EU institutions, and not on the public authorities of the Member States? Unfortunately things are not that simple in the complex postmodern European polity. The EU has a legal system of its own, which is distinct from the legal systems of the Member States, but at the same time very much integrated with them. It is the very hallmark of the EU legal system (technically one should speak of the EC legal system) that it is not a branch of traditional international law, which is still very much formally separated from the domestic laws of states, but that it is intertwined and interconnected with those domestic laws, through a variety of legal and institutional mechanisms, including for example the legal concepts of direct effect and supremacy. This means that it is hardly tenable to limit the Charter to action by the EU institutions as such. For one thing, EU action is as a rule implemented at the level of Member States by the public authorities of those States. Much of the EU's activities consists of general normative action, which needs to be given effect at the level of Member States. An EU Charter of Fundamental Rights could not be fully effective if it were confined to the EU's institutions and did not apply to action by a State's public authorities which implements EU norms.

But where does one draw the line then? When and up to which point are public authorities acting in an EU law context, for the purpose of triggering the EU system of fundamental rights protection, and from which point onwards is that no longer the case? Those questions are difficult to resolve and of huge import for the application and effect of the Charter, especially if it were made legally binding. Again an example, based on past practice of the European Court of Justice, may illustrate the difficulties. As was mentioned, the Court has for a long time safeguarded the protection of fundamental rights through driving the legal vehicle of general principles of EC law. At one stage, the Court decided that those general principles also apply where Member States implement EC legislation. For instance, the way in which Germany had implemented an EC agricultural regulation providing for compensation of farmers in the milk production sector was scrutinised by the Court, and was found to be contrary to EC standards of fundamental rights protection.[9] However, as to general fundamental rights protection the Court has not gone any further than that, whereas it has gone further when applying the principle of non-discrimination on grounds of nationality - which is, of course, also in the nature of a fundamental right, but one which is expressly provided in the EC Treaty. Article 12 of that Treaty provides that there can be no discrimination on grounds of nationality 'within the scope of application of the Treaty'. The latter clause, interestingly enough, is interpreted more broadly than is the concept of implementation of EC legislation. For example, the Court decided that Article 12 applied in criminal proceedings brought in Italy against a German and an Austrian citizen - the charges were drunken driving and the carrying of a prohibited knife respectively - merely on the basis that those citizens were enjoying the free movement of persons in the EU at the time of the acts. The discrimination issue in the case was the use of languages, but that issue itself was in no way connected to any form of EU action.[10] Arguably, the accused could not have relied on fundamental rights as general principles of EC law, because their case did not concern implementation of EC legislation; but they were able to rely on the principle of non-discrimination on grounds of nationality, because that principle applies within the scope of application of the EC Treaty, and because the Court broadly construed that notion.

What is the approach of the Charter? Article 51(1) provides that the provisions of the Charter are addressed to the institutions and bodies of the European Union and to the Member States 'only when they are implementing Union law'. The possible interpretations of that clause could easily form the subject of a PhD thesis, but it does seem that the intention at least is to confirm the current approach of the European Courts towards the scope of fundamental rights as general principles of EC law, as referred to above. An approach which covers fewer forms of action by Member States than are covered by the phrase 'within the scope of application of the Treaty' in Article 12 TEC. But this does not mean that there will be few instances of Member State action which will be covered by the Charter. Again just an example. The EC Treaty, in its version post-Amsterdam, provides for some level of harmonisation of the policies of EU Member States in the field of asylum. The programme of legislative harmonisation which the EU has set out to realise is by no means insignificant, and covers the main elements of asylum law. How then will the

Charter apply once this programme is completed? Will it be arguable that any decision in any asylum case in any Member State contains an element of implementation of EU law in the matter, and that therefore any asylum seeker may invoke the protection of the Charter? If that were the case, it would mean that the whole field of asylum action would be covered by the Charter. It would also mean that any court or tribunal in the EU hearing an asylum case could make a reference under Article 234 TEC to the European Court of Justice in Luxembourg, and that that Court would become Europe's supreme court in asylum cases.

Asylum policies are just one example. As EU legislative action is expanding, so is the scope of the Charter in terms of its effects on action by public authorities of the Member States. However, even with such further expansion the draft Charter harbours an enormous paradox, which in future years may well turn out to be a hinge on which the very character of the European Union may turn. The paradox is the following: The draft Charter contains a substantial number of provisions, primarily in the social policy field, which seem to make little or no sense unless they are made generally binding for the Member States. The rights of workers, for example, are hardly relevant for a Charter which is confined to action by the EU institutions, and does not extend to action by Member States; the effect of those rights would be limited to the EU institutions' own staff. This is not to say that EU employees are not deserving of social protection, but one does not need a general Charter of Fundamental Rights, advertised as a major step forward for EU citizens, to achieve such social protection. Admittedly, the draft Charter is not confined, as explained above, to action by the EU institutions; it also covers action by Member States where they implement EU law. But that renders the paradox even sharper perhaps. For example, Article 30 of the Charter concerns the right of every worker to protection against unjustified dismissal. This provision would only apply where a Member State is implementing EU law.

That would mean that, where a worker has been unjustifiably dismissed, but where he or she cannot show that such dismissal was in the context of implementation of EU law, the Charter would not apply. The protection on unjustified dismissal might therefore depend on the, for the worker presumably completely irrelevant, factor of whether there is an EU law element present. In the longer term, such an approach is clearly untenable, and probably in itself in breach of the fundamental right to equal treatment. At some stage, therefore, the EU will have to decide on whether it takes its own rights language seriously and on whether it makes the rights in the Charter generally binding. The outcome may be that the EU becomes a general vehicle for rights protection, to a much larger extent perhaps than is currently envisaged.

Notes

[1] On the basis of the draft of the Charter of 28 July 2000 (CHARTE 4422/ 00, available on the Europa web site). *Editor's note: Article numbers have been changed to final draft (CHARTE 4487/00 of 28 September 2000).*

[2] I leave aside the question whether there would be incorporation in the EC or EU Treaty.

[3] See further below on this particular aspect.

[4] See the contribution by Meehan for further details.

[5] See for an overview Craig, Paul and Graínne de Búrca. *EU Law – Text, Cases and Materials.* Oxford University Press, 1999[2]. pp. 337-347.

[6] See the comments by Mr Vaz, UK Minister for Europe, before the House of Lords' Select Committee on the European Union, see House of Lords Select Committee on the European Communities. 'The EU Charter of Fundamental Rights'. Session 1999-2000, 8th Report, paragraph 47.

[7] Alston, P. and J.H.H. Weiler. 'An 'Ever Closer Union' in Need of a Human Rights Policy: The European Union and Human Rights'. in: Alston, P. (ed). *The EU and Human Rights.* Oxford University Press, 1999. p.13.

[8] The European Parliament is of course generally elected, but it forms only one part of the EU's legislature; and there is no central government with a majority in parliament.

[9] See Case 5/88, *Wachauf* [1989] ECR 2609.

[10] Case C-274/96, *Bickel and Franz* [1998] ECR I-7637.

Chapter 9

Through the Looking Glass: Making Visible Rights Real

Jonathan Cooper and Róisín Pillay

This chapter argues that there is at present a lack of binding human rights standards and an effective system of remedies for rights violations in the EU and that it is therefore of crucial importance for the EU to accede to the ECHR. Accepting the ECtHR as the supreme human rights court would ensure consistency between the national and EU legal systems and prevent diverging standards and contradictory interpretations between the ECJ and ECtHR jurisprudence. Accession and EU Charter are not, however, mutually exclusive. The Charter is seen as a valuable opportunity to enhance fundamental rights protection within the EU. For it to be most effective it should afford binding and justiciable status at least to basic civil and political rights, but other non-judicial means of enforcement should also be introduced.

The development of the draft European Union (EU) Charter of Fundamental Rights is now well advanced, and it seems certain that a Charter of Rights will, in some form, be put in place. Although the value of the Charter in human rights terms will depend upon its status and scope of application, the drawing up of an EU catalogue of rights is, in principle, to be welcomed. It presents a significant opportunity not only to remedy the lack of binding human rights standards in the EU, but also to build and improve on existing human rights standards.

One regrettable aspect of the debate accompanying the rapid development of the Charter is that it has not been wholly centred on the Charter's effectiveness as an instrument of human rights protection. The proposed Charter has raised questions of expanding EU competences, and has been seen as an instrument of EU nation-building. The Charter has also been represented as a means of enhancing the visibility of rights within the Union, without adding to the substantive legal protection afforded to them. But the crucial question about the Charter is not whether it can or will be used for unacknowledged political objectives, but how far it can achieve the objective of any human rights instrument, and the objective cited in the Preamble to the current draft Charter: enhancing the protection of fundamental rights.[1]

As will be discussed below, there is a clear and identifiable need for effective human rights protection within the EU. In recent months, the Charter has become the catalyst for discussion of how human rights can best be protected within the EU legal system. The criticisms made of the Charter have reignited a wider debate on the steps that need to be taken to effectively protect human rights within the European legal system. In the UK, the Report of the House of Lords European Union Committee on the Charter has helped to ensure that the focus of the debate is a broad one, going beyond the issues of how the Charter should be drafted, to look at how the deficiencies in EU human rights protection can best be rectified, whether by a Charter or by other means.[2] Following a lengthy process of consultation and hearings, the Committee concluded that the most effective measure that could be taken to ensure greater human rights protection would be, not the development of an EU Charter of Rights, but the accession of the EU to the European Convention on Human Rights (ECHR).

Accession, the Committee concluded, would best 'fill the gap' in EU human rights protection.[3] This is a conclusion which JUSTICE supports: it has long been JUSTICE policy that the EU should accede to the ECHR.[4]

The 'gap' in EU human rights protection

Following the publication of the House of Lords European Union Committee Report on the Charter, the House of Lords debated its contents. In rejecting the option of ECHR accession, the UK government has argued that there is no human rights deficit within the EU, and that ECHR standards are sufficiently effective within the Union to redress any gaps in human rights protection.[5]

The view that further binding human rights guarantees are not necessary for effective protection of human rights in the EU is based on the requirements of Article 6(2) of the TEU. Article 6(2) states

'The Union shall respect fundamental rights, as guaranteed by the European Convention for the Protection of Human Rights and Fundamental Freedoms signed in Rome on 4 November 1950 and as they result form the constitutional traditions common to the Member States, as general principles of Community law.'

This provision is justiciable to a limited extent under Article 46(d) TEU.[6]

These provisions have undoubtedly provided a basis for an already growing European Court of Justice (ECJ) jurisprudence on human rights.[7] However, despite the advances made by the Court, the EU legal system currently provides less than satisfactory protection for human rights in a number of respects. The effect of the current system is that there will be many cases in which an individual will not be able to obtain access to the ECJ to allege an infringement of rights, and that even where the matter is raised in court, the individual cannot be assured that sufficient weight will be given to the importance of protecting his or her rights. Furthermore, the lack of a clear catalogue of rights within the Union means that human rights issues arise only at the point of litigation, rather than informing the entire policy development and legislative process.

Critically, there is at present a deficit of human rights protection in relation to EU activity taking place under the Third Pillar, and to a lesser extent activity under Title IV of the EC Treaty, which was formerly under the Third Pillar. Under Article 35 TEU, the jurisdiction of the ECJ does not extend to third-pillar matters. Judicial supervision of visa, asylum and immigration matters under Title IV, is also extremely limited. This lack of judicial supervision and of judicially enforceable human rights standards in these areas is clearly of serious concern. Activity under the Third Pillar and Title IV is particularly human rights sensitive. The inability of the ECJ to regulate and hold accountable, according to human rights standards, activity such as police co-operation, and the operation of databases established under the Schengen Information System and Eurodac, is highly unsatisfactory, and represents a significant gap in the protection of human rights in Europe.

Even in cases falling within the jurisdiction of the ECJ, there remains a human rights deficit. Human rights guarantees do not enjoy sufficient rank within the EU legal system. The low status of human rights standards in the EU system means that they can be overridden by competing Treaty provisions: the ECJ has no jurisdiction to disapply the EC Treaties where they fall short of human rights standards. In the absence of entrenched human rights guarantees at an EU constitutional level, the application of Article 6 TEU by the ECJ cannot ensure effective protection of human rights in the same way as can the European Court of Human Rights, for example, by allowing individuals to bring claims in the certain knowledge that a clear set of human rights standards will be applied and upheld in their case. For example, the Court of Human Rights has, as a matter of Convention law, enforced human rights norms over

EU Treaty provisions, in the recent case of *Mathews v UK*.[8] There, the Court of Human Rights found that the situation under the EU Treaty governing the voting rights of the residents of Gibraltar, violated Article 3 of Protocol 1 of the ECHR. In a case concerning action by the EU institutions, it would seem unlikely that the ECJ could similarly disapply a Treaty provision that conflicted with human rights standards.

Restrictions on individual standing before the ECJ present a real and genuine obstacle to effective enforcement of human rights standards in the Union. The provision in Article 230 TEC that an individual may only challenge a measure of EU law if it 'directly and individually' concerns them, has been interpreted restrictively by the ECJ, making it difficult for individuals to challenge decisions of Community institutions where they infringe their human rights.[9] This sets a practical limitation on the enforceability of human rights, which needs to be addressed in tandem with the preparation of a catalogue of rights such as that in the Charter.

It is the case at present that, however willing the ECJ may be to take a range of human rights standards into account under Article 6 TEU, no written human rights guarantees are directly enforceable in the ECJ. It remains difficult to predict to what extent the Court will take human rights standards into account in any particular case, and to ascertain what standard will be applied. There is therefore an absence of reliable human rights protection in the ECJ. Individuals cannot bring a case before the ECJ with any certainty as to whether and how their human rights will be protected by the court. The case of *SPUC v Grogan*[10] is a good example. That case concerned an injunction on the provision of abortion information. The ECJ, though it might have been expected to consider freedom of expression issues and, in particular, Article 10 ECHR, declined to consider that provision, but instead addressed the issue in terms of the freedom to provide services, holding that this freedom was not interfered with. The ECJ's finding contrasts with the decision of the European Court of Human Rights in *Open Door Counselling v Ireland*,[11] that such restrictions did breach Article 10.

The approach of the EU Courts to privacy rights, for example can be contrasted to that of the ECtHR. In the recent case of *LVM and others*,[12] the Court of First Instance, ruling on the intrusive collection of evidence from a corporation's offices, without a judicial warrant and without the presence of an independent observer, declined to extend the protection of Article 8 ECHR to the applicant in the case. In taking this approach the Court expressly refused to follow the jurisprudence of the ECtHR which held, in *Niemitz v Germany*,[13] that Article 8 ECHR protection of private life, of the home and correspondence did extend to professional or business activities or premises.

This certainty gap in EU human rights protection undoubtedly calls for the identification of a single, clear catalogue of rights which will be enforceable within the EU legal system. Whether the EU Charter will be sufficient to achieve this alone, or whether there is a need for ECHR accession is, however, still a matter of considerable doubt.

ECHR accession

The benefits of the ECHR as a basis for human rights protection within the EU are clear. For 50 years the ECHR has been the focus of the protection of civil and political rights in Europe. Its provisions have gained considerable authority and legitimacy through their application, interpretation and development by the Court (and formerly the Commission) of Human Rights in Strasbourg, by national courts, and also by the ECJ.

Crucially, EU accession to the ECHR would ensure consistency in the protection of human rights in Europe, holding EU institutions to the same standards against which the actions of its Member States, and other European states, are measured. It is certainly a significant anomaly in European human rights protection, that although all Member States of the EU are bound to comply with the standards set out in the ECHR, and indeed ratification of the ECHR is a condition of EU membership, the EU institutions themselves are not clearly bound by the Convention. ECHR accession would ensure consistency between these many national legal systems and the jurisprudence of the ECJ. It would evade many of the practical difficulties of conflict and divergence associated with twin systems of European human rights protection, where an EU Charter operated in parallel to the ECHR. Were the EU to accede to the Convention, then decisions of the ECJ on matters involving Convention rights would, as with decisions of the superior courts in Council of Europe member states, be subject to the supervision of the European Court of Human Rights. The integration of the ECJ within the ECHR system for the protection of human rights would avert the risk of diverging standards and interpretations between the two court systems. It would make the ECJ accountable to the ECtHR in the same way as the superior courts of ECHR states are accountable to it.

Undoubtedly, as has been pointed out in the parliamentary debates following the Report of the House of Lords Committee on the Charter, there are legal and technical difficulties associated with ECHR accession. These difficulties were underlined by the finding of the ECJ in *Opinion 2/94*, that the EC could not become a party to the ECHR without amendments to the Treaties.[14] Further difficulties might arise in relation to the accession of the EU, as opposed to only the EC, to the ECHR, given the doubts as to whether the EU possesses international legal personality. It is also likely that EU accession would necessitate amendment of the ECHR, to be agreed by all member states of the Council of Europe.[15] However, it is likely that these technical difficulties could be overcome. When considered in the light of the legal difficulties associated with an enforceable EU Charter of Rights, they do not provide a basis for rejection of the ECHR option.

Looking beyond the borders of the EU, a further advantage of ECHR accession is that it will ensure consistency in the standard of human rights protection as between EU Member States and other European states. Depending on the extent to which a new Charter would apply to Member State action, the creation of a new Charter could give rise to a two-tier system of human rights protection in Europe, where human rights protection in EU Member States would centre on the ECJ, and the ECtHR would be left to deal mainly with non-EU Member States, primarily in Eastern Europe.

A shift in the focus of human rights protection from the Council of Europe to the narrower forum of the EU, could have a negative effect on the protection of human rights in non-EU states that are members of the Council of Europe. Centring human rights protection for EU states in the ECJ could be seen as creating one standard for Western European EU states, and another for the predominantly Eastern European non-EU members of the Council of Europe. This two-tier system would be avoided by EU accession to the ECHR, whether or not accompanied by the adoption of an EU-specific Charter of Rights. Accession by the EU to the ECHR would ensure that there remains a consistent and authoritative standard of human rights protection throughout Europe.

As we have argued above, it is of crucial importance that the EU should accede to the European Convention on Human Rights. Accession, and the development of a new Charter are not mutually exclusive options, however, and the issue of ECHR accession should remain on the agenda, even following the adoption of a Charter.

The role of a new Charter

Turning to the Charter itself, as its drafting makes rapid progress, it must be considered how, regardless of the question of ECHR accession, the Charter can be made most effective in filling the many current gaps in EU human rights protection. It is unclear, at this stage, just how tangible the benefits of the Charter will be. Although the content of the Charter is taking shape under the auspices of the EU drafting body, the Convention, there are clearly competing visions in relation to the enforceability of the Charter, and in relation to its scope of application. The UK's government continues to adhere to the idea of the Charter as pledge card, as a promoter of the 'visibility' of rights.[16] This is an idea which must be viewed with some scepticism from the perspective of human rights. Whilst increased 'visibility' of rights is an indirect and inevitable side product of the development of rights guarantees that are real and effective, the assumption that visibility is an end in itself carries the danger of ineffectiveness. Rights that are vindicated are inherently visible; but the goal should be the substantive protection of human rights. How, then, could the Charter best take real effect?

Preventing human rights violations: a binding or a declaratory Charter?

At this stage in the Charter's development, it remains uncertain whether and to what extent the Charter will be enforceable in the courts. It is clear that a Charter fully enforceable in the ECJ would, in contrast to a purely declaratory Charter, offer the more reliable mechanism for the protection of human rights in the EU. Effective protection of human rights might also, to some extent, be assisted by a declaratory Charter that took some effect in the courts through Article 6 TEU, as an expression of the 'general principles of Community law' to be applied by the ECJ. A declaratory Charter taking effect through Article 6 would be likely to strengthen the ability of the ECJ to protect rights, by providing a clear set of human rights standards, but the present lack of certainty would remain, in the absence of expressly justiciable guarantees of rights.

The importance of rights that are justiciable before the courts is illustrated by the UK experience leading up to the enactment of the Human Rights Act 1998. Whilst the UK had been party to the ECHR since its inception, the inability of individuals to litigate its provisions before the domestic courts meant that human rights standards were insufficiently enforceable in the UK, despite the possibility of recourse to the Strasbourg Court. Although non-justiciable human rights instruments may have some value, there is ultimately a need for effective enforcement mechanisms.

A new catalogue of judicially enforceable rights, operating alongside the ECHR and national legal systems of human rights protection, is, however, potentially problematic. There would be an increased possibility of ECJ decisions on issues affecting fundamental rights that would be at variance with decisions of the European Court of Human Rights. National courts would then be left to cope with these contradictory authorities. This potential for conflict highlights the need for coherence between European systems for human rights protection, and the importance of EU adherence to the ECHR, which would allow the decisions of the ECJ on matters concerning fundamental rights to be subject to review by the European Court of Human Rights, in common with the decisions of the national courts of European states.

Application in the courts is not the only means by which the Charter can take effect. The application of the Charter in the courts is certainly the first and most important way in which the Charter may have an impact on human rights in Europe. The second is less obvious, and relates to the prevention of breaches of human rights rather than their redress. It should be ensured that the Charter takes effect not only in the courts, but also in the other institutions of the EU, where policy is formulated, legislation prepared, and administrative decisions are taken. It will be important for the Charter to influence the workings of all institutions of the Community, at the early stages of policy formulation and decision-making, and before human rights breaches occur and are litigated in the courts. In this way the Charter could become the catalyst for a culture of rights within the EU.

One important aspect of this broad-based protection of rights under the Charter must be the establishment of non-judicial mechanisms of human rights protection to facilitate and support the Charter. The establishment of a Human Rights Commission or similar body within the EU, which could both monitor the implementation of Charter human rights standards by EU institutions, and provide support to those institutions through the provision of information and assistance in complying with Charter standards, would be a key enforcement mechanism which could considerably enhance the efficacy of the Charter as a mechanism for human rights protection.

The first and most important role of the Charter must be to fill the current gap in EU human rights protection by the effective protection of basic civil and political rights, through the courts and throughout the EU institutions. However, the current draft Charter also looks beyond these rights to social and economic rights. The question then arises whether all of the rights in the Charter should be enforceable in the courts, or whether justiciability should be confined to civil and political rights, or to civil and political rights along with a limited number of social and economic rights. Although many social and economic rights can be and are justiciable, in the EU legal system and elsewhere, the extension of justiciability to new social and economic rights is often seen as a controversial intrusion into matters of public policy, and in the context of the EU Charter, as an attempt to extend the competences of the Union. The present draft of the Charter includes some social and economic rights, though it is a less comprehensive catalogue than that, for example, in the Council of Europe's European Social Charter.

The draft Charter's provisions protect, amongst other things, the right to health care, the right to social security and social assistance and the right to consumer protection. These rights are formulated narrowly however, with reference to the existing national law: Article 33 (now 35), for example, which protects the right to health care, states that

> 'everyone has the right of access to preventive health care and the right to benefit from medical treatment under the conditions established by national laws and practices.'

Many of the workplace rights guaranteed in Chapter IV of the draft Charter, such as workers' rights to information and consultation within an undertaking, and the right of employers and workers to negotiate and conclude collective agreements and take collective action to defend their interests, are also limited by the stipulation that they must be exercised 'in accordance with Community law and national laws and practices.' Since these provisions would seem to be designed to affirm current protections rather than to extend them, their justiciability under the Charter should not be problematic.

Several of the rights included in the draft Charter do seem, at least at first glance, to be aspirational in character and of doubtful justiciability. Article 16, for example, states simply that 'the freedom to conduct a business is recognised.' Article 15(1) states that 'to earn a living, everyone has the right to engage in a freely chosen occupation.' Even more generally, Article 31 (now 33) recognises that 'everyone shall have the right to reconcile their family and professional lives [...]' though the provision goes on to provide for specific circumstances in which this right will apply, for example to protect from dismissal on grounds of pregnancy. It may be that provisions such as these would be best enforced through non-judicial mechanisms. In relation to all of these rights, the establishment of effective non-judicial mechanisms for the protection of human rights should ensure that they will be given some real effect, even if they are not considered to be directly justiciable in the courts.

The scope of application of the Charter

A further issue that remains unresolved, but that will be a key factor in determining the efficacy or otherwise of the Charter, is the extent of its application to EU and Member State activity. It is as yet unclear whether the Charter will apply beyond actions of the EC institutions, to some or all actions of Member States. It would seem realistic to assume that a Charter will take effect most easily in relation to EU institutions. It is certainly in this respect that the least legal difficulty will be created, as application of the Charter to Member State action raises questions as to conflict with other judicial structures, as well as issues of the extent of EU competence. However, a Charter, even a binding one, that was confined to action of the European Community institutions, and did not apply to EU action under the Third Pillar, would leave some of the most problematic areas of EU activity in human rights terms excluded from review. For example, Community customs controls are imposed by officials of the Member States, as are the Title IV controls on immigration and asylum. To leave individuals without the protection of human rights standards in such matters would considerably limit the utility of the Charter. The application of the Charter should therefore be extended to all pillars (although it may be appropriate to allow for different levels of supervision under the Second Pillar).

The content of the Charter and its interpretation

The drafting of the Charter does present an opportunity to advance and develop human rights standards beyond those in existing instruments, and the current draft of the Charter takes some advantage of this. A number of provisions of the Charter are notable for their welcome progression of ECHR and other international standards. Article 19(2), in particular, appears to advance the protection offered by the ECHR in relation to the expulsion or extradition of individuals who will face the death penalty abroad. It provides that

'no one may be removed, expelled or extradited to a State where he could be subjected to the death penalty, torture or other inhuman or degrading treatment.'

Although the ECtHR has accepted, since the *Soering* case,[17] that it will be a breach of the Convention to extradite an individual to face torture, or inhuman or degrading treatment or punishment, such as detention on death row, it has not as yet been accepted by the Strasbourg court that extradition to face the death penalty in itself breaches an individual's Convention rights. The impact of Article 1 of Protocol 6, which prohibits the imposition of the death penalty, on extradition to face the death penalty abroad, has yet to be decided. Although the ECtHR may in the future apply Article 1 of Protocol 6 to prevent extradition in such cases,[18] the text of the Charter provides clear and enhanced protection in this regard, and highlights the potential of the Charter to advance human rights standards in Europe.

It is also notable that the current draft Charter responds to recent scientific developments, for example in Article 3, which protects the right to physical integrity. Article 3(2) provides for specific protection, such as the prohibition of eugenic practices, and the prohibition of the reproductive cloning of human beings. Although Article 8 of the ECHR would provide a general framework within which to deal with these matters, the Charter has the advantage of providing specific protection in relation to them. The draft Charter also includes specific protections for the rights of children (Article 23 (now 24)), a notable omission from the ECHR.

The civil and political rights which form the core of the new Charter are, broadly, similar to those protected under the ECHR. However, in many instances the wording of the rights differs, raising concerns as to possible divergence and conflict between the ECJ and ECHR systems of protection. Draft Article 50(3) (now 52(3)) sets out to address this by providing that the rights in the Charter are to be construed in accordance with the ECHR except where the Charter gives greater protection to rights than that in the ECHR. This provision is welcome, but begs the question as to why it was necessary to depart from the wording of the ECHR in the first place, since, with some exceptions, the majority of the rights as guaranteed in the draft Charter are not protected to an obviously higher level than in the ECHR, but are merely somewhat differently worded. Although the way rights will be guaranteed under the Charter may not differ significantly from the ECHR, there is the possibility that the subtleties of the distinct wording of the Charter may allow for different balances of rights to those struck by the ECtHR under the Convention. Once again, the need for the Charter to be applied within the ECHR legal system, and for EU accession to the ECHR, is highlighted.

Conclusion

The proposed Charter offers an opportunity to ensure the legitimate constraint of EU powers, rather than a pretext to extend them. It is right and necessary that the EU, in common with all European states, should have its actions constrained by clear, enforceable human rights standards. Since the EU legal system does not, at present, sufficiently provide such standards, the drafting of the EU Charter affords a potentially valuable opportunity to at least begin to fill the gaps in EU human rights protection, and it is to be hoped and expected that the development of the Charter is evidence of a real and increasing commitment to human rights within the EU. It is important that the Charter should be viewed not merely as an opportunity to increase the 'visibility' of rights within the Union, but as a means to afford real protection to individuals where it is most needed. The Charter will be most valuable in achieving this if it can be afforded binding and justiciable status, at least in relation to the majority of civil and political rights it protects, and if it can operate in relation to all EU activity under all three pillars, including actions by Member States in the implementation of EU measures.

The preparation of a new European human rights instrument, some 50 years after the drafting of the ECHR, also provides a valuable opportunity to enhance human rights standards, and to advance human rights protection to take account of developments in society and of technological advances. However, the first and most essential aim of the Charter must be to ensure that basic civil and political rights are given sufficient protection within the EU. To ensure coherence, the wording of the civil and political rights guaranteed should follow that of the ECHR to the greatest extent possible.

Valuable though the Charter may be, it cannot be seen as a panacea for the EU's human rights difficulties. Accession to the ECHR remains the most desirable and potentially the most effective means by which the gap in EU human rights protection can be filled, and the EU legal system brought into line with the national legal systems of Europe. If the final agreement reached at the end of this year is on a declaratory rather than a binding Charter, then the question of ECHR accession will remain particularly pressing. However, whatever the status of the Charter, it should be viewed as a step towards ECHR accession, rather than a substitute for it. It is to be hoped that the human rights debate surrounding the Charter will ensure that the issue of EU accession to the ECHR remains on the agenda.

Notes

[1] Draft Charter of Fundamental Rights, Presidency Note, Brussels, 28 July 2000, Charte 4422/00. *Editor's note: Article numbers have been changed to final draft (CHARTE 4487/00 of 28 September 2000).*

[2] House of Lords Select Committee on the European Communities. The EU Charter of Fundamental Rights' Session 1999-2000, 8th Report.

[3] Ibid., para 154. The Committee's conclusion stated that: 'Accession to the ECHR remains the crucial step required if the gap is to be closed. Accession of the EU to the ECHR, enabling the Strasbourg Court to act as an external final authority in the field of human rights would go a long way in guaranteeing a firm and consistent foundation for fundamental rights in the Union. It would secure the ECHR as the common code of Europe. The question of accession by the Union to the ECHR should be on the agenda for the IGC.'

[4] See the JUSTICE Reports The democratic deficit: democratic accountability and the European Union (1996); Judging the European Union: Judicial Accountability and Human Rights (1996) and The Union Divided: Race Discrimination and Third Country Nationals in the EU (1996).

[5] Baroness Scotland, House of Lords, Hansard, 16 June 2000, col. 1906.

[6] Article 46(d) brings Article 6(2) within the jurisdiction of the ECJ 'with regard to the action of the institutions', insofar as the Court has jurisdiction under EC Treaty and the TEU.

[7] The ECJ has a long record of taking human rights standards into account, since the 1970s: Case 11/70, *Internationale Handelsgesellschaft* [1970] ECR 1125; Case 4/73, *Nold* [1974] ECR 491; Case 44/79, *Hauer* [1979] ECR 3727. The Maastricht Treaty of 1993 (Article F2) reflected the ECJ's development of human rights principles, and protection was further advanced in the Amsterdam Treaty.

[8] (1999) 28 EHRR 361.

[9] See generally, Craig, Paul and Gráinne de Búrca. *EU Law: Text, Cases and Materials.* Oxford University Press, 1999^2. chapter 11.

[10] [1991] ECR I-4685.

[11] Series A No 124.

[12] Joined cases T-305/94 a.o., *Limburgse Vinyl Maatschappij a.o.* v *Commission*, n.y.r., [1999] ECR II-931, paras 419-420. The Court held '[t]he fact that the case-law of the European Court of Human Rights concerning the applicability of Article 8 of the ECHR to legal persons has evolved since the judgements in Hoechst, Dow Benelux and Dow Chemical Ibérica [...] has no direct impact on the merits of the solutions adopted in those cases.'

[13] 16 EHRR 97.

[14] In Opinion 2/94 the court stated: '[n]o treaty provision confers on the Community institutions any general power to enact rules on human rights or to conclude international conventions in this field.' The Court went on to consider whether incorporation of the ECHR would be allowed for under Article 308 (then 235) of the Treaty, which grants the community institutions power to act, even where they have no express or implied power to do so,

where such a power would be necessary to enable the Community to carry out its functions with a view to attaining one of the objectives laid down by the Treaty. It found, however, that Article 235, 'being an integral part of an institutional system based on the principle of conferred powers, cannot serve as a basis for widening the scope of Community powers beyond the general framework created by the provisions of the treaty as a whole and, in particular, by those that define the tasks and the activities of the Community. On any view, Article 235 cannot be used as a basis for the adoption of provisions whose effect would, in substance, be to amend the Treaty without following the procedure which it provides for that purpose.'

[15] At present, all Contracting Parties to the ECHR must be Member States of the Council of Europe.

[16] The June 1999 European Council meeting in Cologne based its initiative for the development of a European Union Charter of rights on the need to consolidate the rights applicable within the EU as well as to make 'their overriding importance and relevance more visible to the Union's citizens.'

[17] *Soering v UK* 11 EHRR 439.

[18] Reid, Karen. *A Practitioner's Guide to the European Convention on Human Rights.* 1998. p.221.

Chapter 10

The EU Charter on Fundamental Rights – The Place of the Environment

Clare Coffey

Focusing on environmental rights, this chapter analyses how these are pronounced and afforded protection in international, European and national law and how their promotion is tied in with individual and collective human rights. Whereas substantive environmental rights are largely absent from the EU Treaties, procedural, participatory and information rights have been developed in EU legislation and policy as well as by the ECJ's case-law. It is argued that access to justice for individuals alleging violations of such rights or claiming damages is still somewhat insufficient at present. The EC does, however, consider environmental protection to be a fundamental issue and one of its primary aims. It would therefore seem appropriate to give environmental rights constitutional force. As environmental protection needs to be balanced against other fundamental objectives, the provision in the Charter of legally enforceable substantive rights is seen as problematic. Enhanced guarantees for participation by European citizens and collective interests in environmental matters are considered more appropriate and have the further advantage of improving the EU's democratic legitimacy.

'Man has the fundamental right to freedom, equality and adequate conditions of life in an environment of a quality that permits a life of dignity and well-being'[1]

The idea of bestowing on individuals rights to a certain quality of environment is expressed in several environmental and human rights instruments, including the 1972 Stockholm Declaration on the Human Environment. The Rio Declaration, resulting from the 1992 UN Conference on Environment and Development, included a statement that '[...] human beings are entitled to a healthy and productive life in harmony with nature', going on to call for specific rights to participate in environmental decision-making. References to a healthy or similar environment also appear in several international human rights and environmental conventions. They are also increasingly included in national written constitutions.

Behind the promotion of environmental rights is the basic idea that a healthy environment is necessary for the full enjoyment of individual and collective human rights. The European Convention on Human Rights is silent on the environment but several cases have nevertheless been brought presenting environmental problems, such as high noise levels from airports, as potential infringements of the right to privacy. This attempt to derive environmental rights from human rights stems in part from the realisation that disadvantaged or disenfranchised groups in society are often also those facing the greatest environmental problems.

A second and largely separate aspect of the debate is that environmental values are intrinsic to our society and that environmental rights consequently deserve to be protected and given equal status alongside other rights. The relative merits of both arguments are the subject of ongoing debate, as is the question of whether it is desirable at all to press for environmental rights or whether it might be preferable to rely on traditional forms of environmental protection to promote environmental objectives.

130

As the discussions over the nature and content of an EU Charter of Fundamental Rights proceed, this short article provides an overview of existing environmental rights to 'a clean environment' that exist in EU law and, to a lesser extent, national written constitutions. The development of procedural environmental rights are also outlined, with an emphasis on the new Aarhus Convention, followed by a short discussion of some of the issues surrounding the inclusion of environmental rights in the EU Charter.

EU rights to 'a clean environment'?

Some form of 'environmental right' is now to be found in the written constitutions of many countries, particularly the newer constitutions of the former Soviet Union countries. The type of rights range from specific provisions relating to the protection of the environment to, more commonly, more general statements on the environment and duties to protect it. Within the fifteen EU Member States, several constitutions include at least general references to the environment. For example, the Austrian constitution declares itself generally committed to environmental protection but does not establish an individual right. A similar approach is applied in the German constitution which identifies environmental protection as an objective of the State. Portugal and Spain introduce for individuals a right to enjoy a clean environment, with Portugal providing a fundamental environmental right that is placed on a similar basis to that of the right to life and freedom.[2]

Like the constitutions of many EU Member States, the EU Treaties now also refer to the environment and include a dedicated 'Environment Title' (Title XIX) that calls on Community policy to contribute to *inter alia* 'preserving, protecting and improving the quality of the environment' and 'protecting human health' (Article 174 TEC). The 1957 ÉEC Treaty was not conceived for environmental purposes although that did not prevent environmental measures from being adopted on the basis of internal market provisions of the EC Treaty (Article 95, ex Article 100), as well as the 'catch all' clause that was in Article 235 (now 308). However, the 1987 Single European Act and subsequent amendments to the EC Treaty have introduced and refined the legal basis for EC environmental legislation which is now a substantial area of EC law, and which is also a major force driving environmental policies in the Member States. Since 1999, the EC Treaty also includes a specific reference in Article 2 to 'balanced and sustainable development' and 'a high level of protection and improvement of the environment', alongside other fundamental principles such as raising the standard and quality of life, and economic and social cohesion.

Despite these considerable environmental provisions, the EU Treaties are silent on explicitly environmental rights. However, Article 6(2) of the EU Treaty does state that

'[t]he Union shall respect fundamental rights, as guaranteed by the European Convention on Human Rights and Fundamental Freedoms [...] and as they result from constitutional traditions common to the Member States'.

Environmental rights enshrined in national constitutions could therefore be carried over to the EU Treaties. During the last Intergovernmental Conference (IGC) that culminated in the 1999 Amsterdam Treaty there was only limited discussion of the possibility of explicitly incorporating environmental rights into the EU Treaties. In its Opinion on the IGC[3], the Commission had suggested the introduction of the

'[...] right to a healthy environment, and the duty to ensure it, should be included in those provisions of the Treaty affecting the citizen'.

A strengthening of environmental rights was also promoted by Sweden, emphasising the right of citizens to a good environment and improving access to justice. Overall, however, the discussion on environmental rights was not central to the

IGC and environmental rights did not find their way into the Treaty amendments that were eventually agreed.

The absence of substantive environmental rights to 'a clean environment' in the EU may be a reflection of the problems inherent in the concept of such objective-based environmental rights generally. More than one commentator has pointed to the problems in defining adequately the content and scope of such environmental rights and the difficulty in treating environmental rights as inalienable or absolute when in practice environmental protection involves a complex balancing process between social and economic priorities. Viewing environmental issues through a human rights focus is also criticised as being fundamentally anthropocentric. Finally, and importantly, there is a question of whether environmental rights would in fact add anything to what already exists, apart from rhetoric[4], or whether it would be preferable to rely on other types of environmental rights, such as rights to participate in law making, rather than focusing on rights to a certain environmental quality.

Procedural environmental rights

Even where substantive rights to 'a clean environment' have been established in constitutions, the question will arise as to what in practice this means. This question was the subject of a conference organised by IEEP in 1980 in Salzburg at the request of the Austrian Government. The conclusions of the conference were that implementation of 'environmental rights' would likely depend on the existence of certain procedural rights to facilitate environmental protection. Three specific areas were identified at the conference and set out in the resulting Salzburg Declaration[5], covering the right to access information on the environment, the right to participation and the right to recourse to the Courts.

These three 'procedural' environmental rights are important not only as a means of delivering environmental rights to 'a clean environment'. The existence of procedural rights are now widely recognised as being critical in themselves, encouraging better implementation of environmental legislation and, importantly, helping to make legislation and policy more effective. As such, procedural rights are important for delivering environmental objectives, including but not exclusive to the attainment of substantive environmental rights.

The advantage of focusing on procedural rights is that they are also more concrete in nature, and therefore more easily defined and enforced. They also get around the problem of anthropocentricity as procedural rights can be exercised on behalf of the environment. Importantly, the opening up of procedures can also lead to positive ripple effects beyond environmental protection, by contributing to the process of democratisation. Procedural environmental rights are consequently receiving more widespread attention, recently culminating in the signature of a new Convention dedicated to such rights. The Convention, in turn, is driving efforts to strengthen procedural environmental rights in the EU.

The Aarhus Convention on environmental rights

The Third Ministerial 'Environment for Europe' Conference, held in Sofia in 1995, endorsed a set of Guidelines on access to environmental information and public participation in environmental decision-making, in line with Principle 10 of the Rio Declaration. Principle 10 states that environmental issues are best handled with the participation of all concerned citizens, notably through appropriate access to information held by public authorities and opportunities to participate in decision-making.

As a result of the political commitment made at Sofia, negotiations were initiated in the framework of the UN Economic Commission for Europe and resulted in 1999 in the Convention on Access to Information, Public Participation in Decision-Making and Access to Justice in Environmental

Matters (Aarhus Convention). The Convention was widely endorsed, and was immediately signed by the EC and all EU Member States, except Germany.

The Convention, when it enters into force, will require parties to introduce procedures to support the development of substantive environmental rights that are expressed in the Preamble, i.e. that adequate protection of the environment is essential to human well-being and the enjoyment of basic human rights, and that people have the right to live in an environment adequate to their health and well being and the duty to protect and improve the environment for the benefit of present and future generations. To meet these general goals, the Convention sets out the three sets of procedural rights, mirroring those identified in the earlier Salzburg Declaration, as follows:

- detailed rights and obligations are provided in the area of access to environmental information, including time frames for granting information and limited grounds for public authorities to refuse access to certain types of documents;

- a comprehensive public participation procedure is provided for decisions on specific activities having a significant effect on the environment whereby the public is informed and has opportunities to participate in all stages of the procedure and where the outcome of this procedure is to be taken into account in the final decision; and

- provisions ensuring that the public has appropriate access to justice for alleged impairment to its rights on access to information and public participation, as well as access to justice to challenge acts or omissions by private persons and public authorities which contravene provisions of national environmental law.

The Convention is effectively designed to enable civil society to play an active role in protecting and improving the environment for present and future generations, and as such should also strengthen democracy. It is making a major contribution to the international debate on environmental rights and has particular ramifications for the EC since, unlike other conventions, the Aarhus Convention explicitly covers the activities of Community institutions.

Procedural environmental rights in EU law

The EU Treaties do not explicitly confer rights to 'a clean environment' on EU citizens, but it would be wrong to assume that there are no environmental rights arising out of EU law. On the contrary, procedural environmental rights already featured in the 1985 Environmental Impact Assessment (EIA) Directive (85/337) which introduced public rights to access information contained in planning applications that fell within the parameters of the Directive. Since 1985, successive developments have strengthened the level and quality of participation in the development of EC environmental law, as well as in decisions taken in the implementation of EC law in the Member States. The table below highlights key items of EC environmental legislation which introduce procedural environmental rights. These developments have been driven in part by 'ideas of basic freedoms' as well as more practical desires to increase the effectiveness of environmental policy.[6]

Information

Information is essential not only to hold governments accountable, but also to monitor and enforce legislation on the private sector actors. The importance of access to information on the environment was reflected in 1990 with the adoption of the EC Directive 90/313 on freedom of access to information on the environment. The Directive is still the main piece of 'rights-based' EC environmental law and has made an important contribution to introducing a right to information in the EU Member States. Other EC Directives also provide a right of access to information, including Directives on major accidents hazards (known as the Seveso

136

II Directive) (92/82), integrated pollution prevention and control (IPPC) (96/61) and air quality (96/62).

Although Directive 90/313 was used as a template for the information provisions under the Aarhus Convention, the right to access information is not absolute. In particular, there is ambiguity as to the type of documents covered by the Directive and its implementation in the Member States has consequently been subject to legal challenge. A remaining uncertainty is the extent to which information on sectoral activities, for example, subsidies provided to the Member States' fisheries sectors, can be considered as being 'environmental' and therefore subject to the provisions of the Directive. This issue is critical, particularly in the light of the Community's renewed commitment to integrating environmental considerations within sectoral policies, as expressed in Article 6 of the Treaty.

Another key weakness of the existing information provisions is that Community documents are currently excluded from the remit of the Directive, something that will need to be rectified if the EC is to implement the Aarhus Convention. Separate Decisions have been adopted concerning Commission, Council and European Parliament documents (respectively, Decisions 93/731, 94/90 and 97/632), but there are ongoing concerns about the implementation of these. There are also documents, importantly those submitted by the Member States, which are currently not subject to rules of the Community institutions. One of the changes introduced by the Amsterdam Treaty was a specific public right of access to all (not just environmental) Commission, Parliament and Council documents, subject to the principles and conditions to be laid out in secondary legislation by May 2001 (Article 255). Proposals on this issue are now with the Council[7] and new legislation can be expected to follow in due course.

Participation

Information on its own is unlikely to be sufficient to affect the content of legislation, in the absence of opportunities for environmental interests to participate in the policy process. Yet, unlike access to information provisions under EC law, there is no single piece of 'horizontal' legislation to secure participation in decision-making in the EC institutions or in the Member States. Participation is instead restricted to specific areas, notably planning decisions such as those falling within the remit of the Environmental Impact Assessment Directive 85/337, emergency and other plans under the Seveso II Directive 92/82 and decisions relating to industrial permits made under the IPPC Directive 96/61.

The proposed Water Framework Directive, which is nearing adoption after long and arduous negotiations, is set to introduce into EC law some of the most widespread environmental provisions on participation. The proposal includes specific provisions on consultation, requiring Member States to 'encourage the active involvement of all interested parties in the implementation of the Directive'. Apart from making available a series of documents to the public,

> 'Member States are to allow at least six months to comment in writing on those documents in order to allow active involvement and consultation' (Article 14(3)).

These laws seek to secure participation within the Member States' decision-making processes. Participation in decisions by the EC institutions is quite a separate issue. Since 1979, European citizens have had the right to directly elect representatives to the European Parliament while the Parliament's legislative role has also grown so that it now has equal powers to the Council of Ministers in many areas of environmental law-making. While not offering a direct opportunity for citizens to participate in decisions affecting the environment, this clearly represents an important aspect of participation. There are also opportunities for citizens to participate in public hearings and consultation exercises organised by the Parliament.

Environment and business groups have additionally developed a range of informal ways of participating in policy making, in order to further their particular policy objectives. Among these are regular meetings organised by various Directorates General of the Commission to hear the concerns of environmental groups and to discuss possible solutions. The Commission has also established a number of formal advisory committees to represent specific industry or sectoral interests. Increasingly these committees, which include agriculture, fisheries and transport committees, also offer seats to environmental groups and as such present important opportunities to integrate environmental considerations within sectoral policy-making.

Quite separately, DG Environment has pioneered a new approach to developing proposals by setting up specific working groups involving industry and environment representatives. This pattern was applied initially in the so-called 'Auto-oil II' programme which sought to develop EU proposals for fuel and air quality standards. The model has subsequently been modified and applied to the Clean Air for Europe (CAFE) programme also led by DG Environment.

To support *meaningful* participation in these and other fora and discussions, the EU budget offers financial support to European level environmental non-governmental organisations. Despite these various opportunities for participation, the involvement of environmental groups in Advisory Committees offers perhaps the only *right* for participation and even then it would be difficult to argue that legal rights were established for individual citizens to participate directly in the policy process. The Commission has consequently been examining Community legislation which may be affected and which may need to be amended in light of the Aarhus Convention and its provisions on participation, and it remains to be seen whether and, if so, how rights to participation will be improved.[8]

Access to justice

An important corollary of rights to access information and participation is the ability to challenge decisions in court. Member State Governments do have standing to challenge decisions taken by EU institutions in the European Court and the Court of First Instance. Individuals and organisations, by contrast, can only challenge decisions addressed to them or decisions addressed to others which are of 'of direct and individual concern' to them (Article 230 EC Treaty). The issue of standing was highlighted in a challenge against a Commission decision concerning the Structural Funds that was brought by Greenpeace and a group of citizens from the Canary Islands in 1998.[9]

Individuals can also ask for national courts to refer cases to the ECJ for reference, but they must first obtain standing in the national courts and access to justice in environmental matters is not uniformly available in the Member States. Individuals can also formally complain to the Commission if they think EC law is not being implemented properly, although it is the prerogative of the Commission to decide whether to start official proceedings. There are ongoing discussions on developing access to justice in national courts, associated with the possible introduction of an EU civil liability regime. Among the options outlined in the 2000 White Paper on environmental liability[10] is granting environmental interest groups access to national courts if liabilities are not adequately addressed by Member States.

Despite the significance and repeated calls for greater access to justice, the implementation of the Aarhus Convention provisions on access to justice may yet pose the greatest difficulties for the EC and could potentially require amendments to the EC Treaty itself before the EC is ready to ratify it. There are diverging views within EU institutions on this point, with some believing that modification of the Treaty will be needed.

Table Environmental rights in Selected EC legislation[11]

Item of EC Legislation	Procedural rights
Environmental Impact Assessment (EIA) Directive 85/337	Right to participate in decision-making, including access to information relating to applications and decisions.
Contained use of genetically modified micro-organisms (GMMOs) Directive 90/219	Safety information relating to the contained use of GMMOs is to be made publicly available.
Freedom of access to information on the environment Directive 90/313	Individual rights to access environmental information, subject to certain limits.
Major accident hazards (Seveso II) Directive 92/82 (replacing 'Seveso' Directive 82/501)	Public to be consulted on external emergency plans and be able to give an opinion on planning for new developments; information on safety measures and the requisite behaviour in the event of an accident is to be supplied to persons liable to be affected by an emergency; safety reports are also to be publicly available.
Directive on Integrated Pollution Prevention and Control (IPPC) 96/61	Public participation in deciding on IPPC permits; access to information on permits and results of monitoring of releases under the permits, subject to limits set out in 90/313.
Air Quality Framework Directive 96/62	Public access to air quality monitoring results and action plans.
Proposed Water Framework Directive – text agreed in conciliation	Would introduce right to comment on draft and final river basin management plans and access to associated 'background documents and information'.

Item of EC Legislation	Procedural rights
Proposed Strategic Environmental Assessment (SEA) Directive (COM(1999)73)	Draft plans/programmes and final decisions would be publicly available; public would be given early and effective opportunity within appropriate timeframes to comment on draft plans/programmes.
White Paper on Environmental Liability (COM (2000)66)	Suggests public interest groups could be given access to justice, including judicial review and injunctions, and the right to sue polluters for damage.

ECJ case-law - developing procedural rights

In addition to specific environmental rights conferred on citizens by environmental legislation, developments in EC case-law have contributed to the body of EU environmental rights. The European Court of Justice (ECJ) has held that certain provisions of directives are 'directly effective' and consequently give individuals rights which they can rely upon before a national court. To have direct effect, provisions must be sufficiently clear and precise, unconditional and leave no discretion to Member States in their implementation.[12] Where such provisions are directly effective, they will confer rights which can be relied upon against the State and, in specific circumstances, also against other individuals or companies. In general, direct effect only arises where a Member State has failed to implement provisions of a directive properly or at all by a given deadline.[13] Furthermore, its application to environmental cases has been little tested and there is consequent uncertainty as to whether environmental directives which impose general duties, such as setting standards, can be regarded as conferring private rights.[14]

A further important area of case-law relates to rights for damages suffered as a consequence of a Member State breaching its Treaty obligations. According to the Francovich cases[15], a State may be held liable to individuals for loss suffered, although liability is subject to three conditions: a) the result prescribed by the Directive should entail the grant of rights to individuals, b) it should be possible to identify the content of those rights on the basis of the provisions of the Directive and c) there is a causal link between the State's breach and the loss and damage suffered. A breach must also be 'sufficiently serious' in order to give rise to a right[16]. However, this and the direct effect doctrine only confer rights on citizens if they are first able to bring cases to the national court.

Environmental rights in the EU Charter?

Environment is increasingly seen as a fundamental issue facing society in Europe, both as a means of guaranteeing human rights and for its own sake. The EC has included the environment as a primary aim of the EC and developed an extensive legal basis for developing secondary environmental laws, including laws that confer rights on information, participation and, to a lesser extent, access to justice. It would therefore seem appropriate to use discussions on the EU Charter of Fundamental Rights to give environmental rights constitutional force.

However, it is clear that a substantive environmental right to 'a clean environment' is difficult to formulate and enforce. By providing citizens with a substantive right to air or water that meets certain standards, whatever the social, economic or ecological setting, individuals would be able to seek damages or remediation against Member States or public authorities that failed to take the necessary steps to meet the standards. Questions remain as to suitability or legal practicability of introducing such a right, and how this would be balanced against other fundamental rights.

Given the above, it may be preferable to press for the inclusion in the EU Charter of environmental rights which can secure proper *participation* by environmental interests in the development and implementation of EU policies, while also delivering fundamental improvements in the functioning of democratic institutions in Europe. This is all the more relevant and resonant at a time when the EU institutions and the role of citizens is coming under increasing and critical scrutiny. The Charter could therefore set out a right to access to information, participation and justice in matters relating to the environment, as a means of securing a high level of environmental protection.

If such an approach were accepted it would to a large degree reaffirm the developments in EC law that have occurred over the last 15 years, but it would also take on board recent advancements in international environmental law that are reflected in the Aarhus Convention and which the EC and the Member States have signed up to.

Notes

[1] Stockholm Declaration on the Human Environment, 1972.

[2] EEB 1998 Doors to Democracy: current trends and practices in public participation in environmental decision making in Western Europe. Regional Environmental Centre for Central and Eastern Europe, Hungary.

[3] COM(96) 90.

[4] Boyle, A. and M. Anderson M (eds). *Human Rights Approaches to Environmental Protection*. Oxford University Press, 1998.

[5] Published in: Kromarek, P. (ed). *Environnement et droit de l'homme.* UNESCO, 1987.

[6] See Douglas-Scott, S. 'Environmental Rights in the European Union, in Human Rights Approaches to Environmental Protection'. in: Boyle and Anderson, 1998.

[7] COM(2000) 30.

[8] Answer by Mrs Bjerregaard on behalf of the Commission to European Parliament Written Question E-0611/99.

[9] Case C-321/95, *Greenpeace and others v Commission* [1998] ECR I-1651.

[10] COM(2000)66.

[11] For further information on these and other EC environmental legislation, see Haigh (ed) 1992 Manual of Environmental Policy: the EU and Britain, Institute for European Environmental Policy, London. Elsevier Science.

[12] Case 26/62, *Van Gend en Loos v Administratie der Belastingen* [1963] ECR 3.

[13] Haigh (ed) 1992.

[14] Douglas-Scott, 1998.

[15] Cases C-6/90 and C-9/90, *Francovich and Bonifaci v Italy* [1991] ECR I-5357.

[16] Cases C-46/93 and C-48/93 *Brasserie du Pêcheur SA v Federal Republic of Germany and R v Secretary of State for Transport ex parte Factortame and others* [1996] ECR I-1029. See also Haigh (ed) 1992.

Acknowledgments

I wish to thank my colleagues Nigel Haigh and Andrew Farmer for their helpful comments on this paper.

Chapter 11

A Business Perspective on the EU Charter

Frédérique Bosvieux

This chapter discusses some of the issues and controversies surrounding an EU Charter from a business perspective. Business has consistently supported the objective of setting out clearly the fundamental values that all EU Member States share and has called for a declaratory Charter maximising the visibility of existing justiciable fundamental rights and outlining citizens' means of enforcement. Concern is expressed that the Convention with its current draft has gone beyond its original mandate. The inclusion of new enforceable rights is seen as carrying the inherent risk of creating considerable legal uncertainty through conflicts of jurisprudence, shifting the balance of competencies between the EU institutions and the Member States and increasing the political pressure to shift the EU's agenda away from the formerly agreed economic and structural reform agenda.

Introduction

The CBI has consistently supported the objective set at Cologne of drawing up an EU Charter of Fundamental Rights

'to make their overriding importance and relevance more visible to the Union's citizens'.

We believe that there is value in setting out clearly the fundamental values that all EU Member States share at the start of the 21st century, particularly in the context of enlargement.

The CBI has called for a declaratory Charter which sets out existing justiciable fundamental rights and how citizens can enforce them; such an approach will maximise the visibility of fundamental rights to EU citizens, whilst preserving the existing, effective legal mechanisms for rights protection.

However we have become increasingly concerned that the drafting Convention may be straying beyond what was agreed at Cologne. The difficult mandate given to the Convention - to draw up a Charter without a clear view on the likely legal status of the final document - has led to a range of competing models for the Charter being put forward. We believe that proposals for a legally binding Charter which goes beyond existing enforceable rights would:

- create considerable legal uncertainty, through conflicts of jurisprudence between courts at European level and judicial review of existing national and EU legislation;

- shift the balance of competencies between the EU institutions and Member States outside of the normal process of intergovernmental negotiations, breaching the subsidiarity principle; and

- increase the political pressure to shift the EU's agenda away from the economic and structural reform agenda agreed at Lisbon.

This Chapter outlines the CBI's support for a declaratory Charter focusing on those rights which are currently legally justiciable, and sets out the reasons why we believe the alternative models put forward would be damaging to business.

A declaratory Charter setting out rights currently legally enforceable at EU level

The CBI welcomed the European Council's objective of raising EU citizens' awareness of their fundamental rights and their enforcement mechanisms. It will enhance the culture of rights and responsibilities across Europe and will increase the democratic legitimacy of European institutions by ensuring that their actions do not infringe citizens' fundamental rights.

The approach preferred by the CBI and a number of governments, including the UK, is that the Charter should be declaratory and should include only those rights which are already recognised as both fundamental and justiciable.

The Cologne conclusions made it clear that the Convention should consider the inclusion of fundamental rights in all spheres, not just political or civil rights but also economic and social rights, 'in so far as they do not merely establish objectives for action by the Union'. This distinction between fundamental rights and policy objectives is a vital one. The undiscriminating use of the word 'right' in earlier EU texts has caused a lot of confusion; it has been used to describe both justiciable rights - such as those set in the European Convention on Human Rights (ECHR), under which EU citizens can take cases to the Strasbourg Court - and political aspirations which have no legal effect, such as those referred to in the 1961 European Social Charter and the 1989 Community Charter of Fundamental Social Rights of Workers. 'Rights' must either be capable of enforcement in a court of law or be recognised as essentially exhortatory in nature.

The CBI believes that political aspirations, particularly on economic and social issues, must be recognised as such and not given legal status. Otherwise the Charter will become a catalogue of good intentions; including political aspirations which cannot be enforced in the Courts would simply mislead European citizens by offering a chimera of 'rights' which dissolve under scrutiny. Only those fundamental rights that can be enforced through legal process by individual citizens should be set out in the Charter. This means the inclusion of those rights set out in the European Convention on Human Rights, which has been ratified by all EU Member States, along with a number of inalienable rights from the EU Treaties which individuals can use directly as a legal base for bringing cases to the European Court of Justice. In the social field, this includes such rights as the freedom to choose an occupation, the freedom of movement, the right to equal treatment between men and women, the right to freedom of association and the general principle of non-discrimination.

The Charter should be a declaratory document setting out these justiciable rights in clear and simple language for maximum impact and pointing to the appropriate source instrument and existing legal mechanisms by which citizens can enforce these rights.

Such a Charter would be a 'showcase' for the values of the Union and the fundamental legal rights that underpin those values. It would clarify the existing rights system but not undermine it. Nor would it change the legal competences of any of the Union institutions; the European Court of Justice (ECJ) would retain jurisdiction over Treaty rights and the Strasbourg Court of Human Rights would keep its responsibility for ensuring national compliance with the ECHR.

A range of competing models for the Charter have, however, been put forward, based on very different views of what it should achieve. However, the CBI believes that none of these approaches would be appropriate.

A limited Charter incorporated into the EU Treaties?

One approach, supported in particular by the German government and some Scandinavian countries, is for the Charter to be legally binding on the EU legislators and at national level in relation to regulations implementing Directives. They see the scope of the Charter as limited, with an emphasis on political, civil and economic rights already part of the ECHR rather than on the long list of social rights being proposed in other quarters.

Such a view is based on a continuing concern about the lack of democratic accountability of the EU institutions. The argument is that unlike national legislators, the Commission and the Council do not face an effective judicial check on their powers to act in ways which may contravene fundamental human rights. The European Court, it is argued, has never condemned the EU institutions for failing to respect human rights, yet it is far from unusual for member state governments to lose cases before the Strasbourg Court of Human Rights. The Charter, rather than extending the powers of the EU institutions as those calling for a European Constitution would wish, should therefore restrain them from trampling on citizens' rights when they legislate. Like most national constitutions, it would be intended as a set of negative rights that cannot be contravened, rather than positive rights placing requirements on governments and the EU to 'deliver'.

The CBI fully supports the role that a declaratory charter can play in restraining EU institutions from infringing citizens' rights. We believe a declaratory document is quite sufficient to remind EU institutions of their obligations to respect EU citizens' fundamental rights. Although EU law does, in certain circumstances, have direct effect on citizens, EU legislation, after all, mainly impacts on them through implementation in national legislation – such law can already be challenged in the Strasbourg Court. For example an EU directive implemented in the UK in a way which contravened the ECHR would be open to challenge in Strasbourg. Legal protection is therefore already in place against abuse of power by the EU institutions.

As well as being unnecessary, making the Charter legally binding through incorporation into the Treaties would undermine rather than enhance the existing system of rights protection. At present, the European Court of Human Rights in Strasbourg has ultimate responsibility for the protection of the fundamental rights set out in the European Convention of Human Rights. The Charter is very likely to duplicate those rights, but if legally binding, would give jurisdiction for their enforcement to the European Court of Justice in Luxembourg. Overlaps of jurisdiction between the two Courts could cause real confusion and legal uncertainty. And at the political level, it could undermine the Council of Europe.

Confusion would arise over which Court citizens should take their case to. As all EU Member States have signed the ECHR, redress would normally come from Strasbourg once all national avenues had been explored. But the option of going to the European Court of Justice might be more attractive. Typically it takes five years to take a case to Strasbourg, whereas the Luxembourg Court normally rules within two. Equally, the jurisprudence of the ECJ on the same rights might evolve in a different direction from the approaches taken in Strasbourg. The ECJ is known as a harmonising court, liable to follow a purposive approach. Strasbourg by contrast has been careful to produce judgements which are sensitive to different national traditions, allowing different approaches to complying with fundamental rights. Competing rulings between the Strasbourg Court and the ECJ might develop based on different interpretations of the same rights. This would considerably undermine legal certainty: which interpretation should governments and employers follow? Established precedents from Strasbourg which governments know they comply with could be overturned by the ECJ, leaving them needing to review national legislation.

Some have argued that even if the ECHR were incorporated into the Treaty, it would be possible to ensure the precedence of the Strasbourg Court over ECHR rights. It is unclear how this could be achieved given that the European Court of Justice has responsibility for Treaty rights.

Equally, incorporating the Charter into the Treaties would lead to the development of a two-speed system of case-law that would weaken the Council of Europe. The European Court would develop its own body of case-law that would not be applicable to non-EU members of the Council of Europe. The Council of Europe has worked well by integrating into the EU's human rights culture the Eastern European non-EU members. It would send an unfortunate message about the future solidarity of the Council if the EU decided to tackle human rights issues separately and in effect opted-out of the Strasbourg system.

Towards a federal Europe?

Another view, pressed by many trade unions, NGOs and Members of the European Parliament, is that the Charter should be seen as an embryonic EU constitution. They support a legally binding Charter that would be enforced by the ECJ and would have direct effect on both the EU institutions and Member States - by allowing judicial review by the ECJ not just of European Directives and their national implementation, but also of domestic law.

They see a legally recognised constitution as a major step towards building a European state. To quote Andrew Duff, rapporteur on the Charter for the European Parliament:

'The consequence of the Charter installing a fundamental rights regime within the [EU] treaties is part of the federalising process.'[1]

Just as the Supreme Court had a critical role in developing federal power in the US through purposive interpretations of the Constitution, so the federalists believe an EU constitution would act as a driver of integration through the ECJ's jurisprudence, changing the balance of competencies between EU institutions and Member States.

'The Charter is a dynamic project, which will redefine where power lies. The Charter will have consequences for the share out of competency within the Union. The Charter is a means towards the further political reform of the Union'[2].

Supporters of this approach have also lobbied for a broad Charter going beyond existing rights. They have called for the incorporation in a legally binding Charter of a wide range of non-legally binding texts; the 1961 European Social Charter, the 1989 Community Charter of Fundamental Social Rights of Workers and a range of International Labour Organisation Conventions. Equally, they have called for existing rights established in EU legislation, such as maternity rights, to be turned into general and unqualified rights.

The CBI believes that 'rights' such as those set out in the 1961 European Social Charter and the 1989 Community Charter of Fundamental Social Rights of Workers and in ILO Conventions are of a different nature and status to rights which are currently legally enforceable. The 'rights' set out in the EU social charters are political aspirations of the European Union, which have no legal effect. Equally, rights set in ILO Conventions are critically important global minimum standards, which are binding on those Member States that ratify them. But they are not directly justiciable rights which can be enforced by individuals in a court of law and so cannot be compared with the ECHR or the Treaty rights.

These rights should not be incorporated into a legally binding Charter. To do so would shift the balance of power between Member States and the EU outside of the normal process of intergovernmental negotiations. It would also generate considerable legal uncertainty as it is unclear how such 'aspirational' rights could be interpreted in practice by the European Court.

Many of the 'rights' set out in the EU social charters and ILO conventions are in areas which are currently the responsibility of Member States, such as pay, the right to strike, health, education and most areas of employment policy. To incorporate them in a legally binding Charter would allow the European

Court of Justice (ECJ) to carry out judicial review not just of European Directives but also of domestic law. National legislation such as that setting out the parameters of a constitutional right to strike could be struck out on grounds of incompatibility following a more expansive ECJ ruling. This would enlarge the competence of the European institutions by the back door.

Changing the balance of power between Member States and EU institutions by creating new rights and giving them legal value by incorporating the Charter into the Treaties would be an enormous political step. It would not be compatible with the mandate provided at Cologne - which was clear that the Convention's primary role was to consider how to make existing rights more visible. Allowing judicial review at the European level of decisions made by national or local governments would risk taking decisions out of the hands of democratically elected politicians which are rightly their responsibility. Such shifts in sovereignty have major implications and should only be considered through full intergovernmental discussions. Quoting the House of Lords Select Committee on the European Union:

> 'Any attempt to enlarge competence in this way would be highly controversial. The purpose of the Charter should be to protect individuals against infringement of their fundamental rights by the institutions of the EU or by Member States applying Community or EU legislation. To this extent, the Charter could be regarded as restricting the competence of EU institutions'[3].

Incorporating political aspirations and ILO standards into a legally binding Charter would also create considerable legal confusion for business and individual citizens. Such 'aspirational' rights would be almost impossible to interpret in practice by the European Court of Justice, causing real uncertainty for governments and business. For example, how should 'every worker has the right to protection against unjustified dismissal' be interpreted? On the face of it, it seems uncontroversial. But in practice there is no EU legislation that guarantees such a right. And although at national level every member state has rules on unfair dismissal, they vary considerably in terms of qualifying period, compensation available and so on. Equally, it is not clear how a right to 'social assistance and housing benefit in order to ensure a decent existence', a right to access to vocational and continuing training, and a right to strike could be interpreted at EU level given the diversity of national provisions.

The CBI has also resisted calls to turn ordinary employment rights such as maternity rights and certain rights to workers' information and consultation, into legally binding 'fundamental rights' in the Charter. These rights are heavily qualified legislative rights which apply only in specific circumstances. To turn them into unqualified rights would allow cases to be taken to the ECJ arguing that existing directives are incompatible with the requirements of the Charter. For example, it is uncertain whether the Parental Leave Directive would be considered to go far enough towards meeting the broad right of parents to 'reconcile professional and family life' proposed in the latest draft of the Charter. Individual parents or trade unions could take cases to the ECJ arguing that the Directive is insufficient to deliver the much broader right set out in the draft Charter. Such cases would allow the Court to drive an EU legislative agenda.

A legally binding Charter extending existing rights would therefore increase pressure on the Council of Ministers to agree to more legislation to implement these rights. This would effectively turn the Charter into a social action programme - therefore going much beyond the mandate given at Cologne.

A broad declaratory Charter?

A third competing approach is for the Charter to incorporate a wide range of rights, particularly in the social field, but to be declaratory.

The CBI believes that, even in a declaratory form, such a broad Charter would increase political pressure on the Commission and Council to develop a more expansive set of EU legislative proposals in the social field. This was precisely what happened following agreement of the 1989 Social Charter, which set out an expansive range of 'fundamental' social rights of workers. It was not a binding text, but it was used to press for the development of far wider social competences for the Commission. The result, famously, was the Maastricht Social Chapter. The potential political impact of the Charter was made clear by the Commission itself in its latest Social Action Agenda, where it says: 'Equally important for future social policy may be the Charter of Fundamental Rights'[4].

If the Cologne mandate is followed, from a legislative perspective, the Charter should have no impact on EU social policy. But this is clearly not how the Commission or unions see it.

Looking at the draft Charter (Convent 45)[5], a concrete example of the potential political impact of such a broad Charter is that of the proposed right to workers' information and consultation. The inclusion of such a broad and unqualified right in the Charter would pre-empt the current debate over the draft National Information and Consultation Directive. This proposal would require all companies in the EU with more than 50 employees to set up a statutory works council to be consulted on decisions that might impact on employees. It has been rejected by UNICE, and by the UK, German, Danish and Irish Governments on grounds of subsidiarity – it deals with purely national industrial relations issues which are not within the Commission's competence. Article 25 (now 27) of the draft would increase the political pressure on the governments currently constituting the blocking minority to accept the draft directive. A similar issue arises from the proposed 'right to protection in the event of unjustified dismissal' (Article 28, (now 30)). The Commission, in particular, is pushing for its competence in this area to be shifted from a unanimity basis to qualified majority voting. Its argument will be strengthened if the current Article in the Charter is agreed.

The European social agenda should be driven by a clear focus on the most appropriate level and type of action needed to address the various social and employment challenges facing Member States. The Charter should not lead to an extension of EU competences in areas which Council members have previously argued should be left to national law and practice. The Charter should restrain EU institutions from infringing citizens' rights, not act as a licence to legislate.

Conclusion

The impact of the Charter will depend on which of the competing approaches is finally followed. The legal status of the document is clearly the critical factor in the longer term. But even a non-binding Charter could have a significant impact by placing greater pressure on governments to accept an extension of EU level action in areas where it would not be appropriate. And in the meantime such an approach would raise expectations amongst EU citizens of 'rights' which cannot be delivered. The CBI believes that only a declaratory Charter which clearly sets out existing justiciable rights will achieve the objectives set at Cologne.

Whilst the EU's Council of Ministers seems unlikely to agree to anything other than a declaratory document at Nice, we are very concerned that a declaratory compromise would come at a price. A final Charter including new 'fundamental social rights' would create legal confusion and be used as a spur for more legislation. In the long term, if the Charter is incorporated into the Treaty, a judicial impetus for more Commission activity seems inevitable. The constitutional and sovereignty issues this raises are profound.

The CBI will continue to lobby for a declaratory Charter in line with existing justiciable rights.

Notes

[1] *Financial Times*, March 29, 2000, p. 2.

[2] Report on the drafting of a European Union Charter of Fundamental Rights, Committee on Constitutional Affairs, European Parliament, 3 March 2000, A5-0064/2000. Rapporteurs: Andrew Duff; Johannes Voggenhuber.

[3] House of Lords Select Committee on the European Communities. 'The EU Charter of Fundamental Rights'. Session 1999-2000, 8th Report.

[4] COM(2000) 379, Communication from the Commission to the Council, the European Parliament, the Economic and Social Committee and the Committee of the Regions, *Social Policy Agenda.*

[5] *Editor's note: Article numbers have been changed to final draft (CHARTE 4487/00 of 28 September 2000).*

Chapter 12

Social Rights Protection in the European Union – The Trade Union Perspective

David Feickert

Commenting from a trade union perspective, this chapter focuses on the development of social rights from the Community Charter to the Social Chapter and now the EU Charter. The advancement of economic and social rights in the EU is discussed in the wider context of the EU's progression from a Europe for business to a people's Europe - a Europe where market forces and the effects of globalisation are balanced by a European social model built aiming at sustainable growth and social cohesion. European trade unions have stressed the indivisibility of human rights and have long campaigned for a document containing rights at work, civil and political rights, citizenship rights, rights for third-country nationals, social and economic rights, binding political objectives and programmatic rights. The importance of social rights is exemplified, in particular, by reference to information and consultation rights, the right to strike, and collective bargaining. A Charter, if incorporated into the Treaties and legally binding, is welcomed as an opportunity to make real progress towards a people's Europe by reinforcing the faith of citizens in the social bargain and an EU which affords clear, coherent and effective protection of their individual rights.

The TUC has argued consistently that we should be at the heart of Europe. This means that Britain should be at the heart of Europe. The trade unions should be at the heart of Europe and fundamental rights should be there, too, at the centre. The European vision and the European model have their critics, not least in Britain. Many of these critics do not believe in the European social model. Some of them believe in a free trade area but reject UK membership of the single currency. Others support both the single market and the euro but reject any significant EU involvement in economic and social rights. They seem to believe that the European case can be won on the basis of the business agenda alone.

To the extent to which their argument often dominates the debate, they are obviously wrong. According to the polls, Euroscepticism is increasing in Britain. We need to face up to the fact that you will not shift public opinion on Europe on the slogan of a Europe for business. It must be a people's Europe, too. This is why the campaign for the Charter of Fundamental rights is important. In the TUC, the last European campaign for fundamental rights, which led to the Community Charter of the Fundamental Social Rights of Workers (Community Charter) and the Social Protocol and Agreement (now incorporated into the EC Treaty's Social Chapter), is etched on our minds. It has become an indelible part of our history.

Community Charter

It is well known that Mrs Thatcher was a passionate opponent of European social rights. She was not very pleased when we invited Jacques Delors, the former European Commission President, to our Congress in September 1988. He came to speak about the Community Charter of Social Rights. The origins of the Community Charter reveal just how closely European trade unions have been involved in the campaign for fundamental rights. The Charter was actually the product of an undertaking made by Jacques Delors in the keynote speech to the ETUC Congress, held earlier in May 1988, in Stockholm.

Jacques Delors said that he would press the heads of government at the Summit in Hanover in June to ensure that there was a social dimension to the Single Market. He made three proposals at the ETUC Congress which were, first, a platform of guaranteed social rights containing general principles, such as every worker's right to be covered by a collective agreement, and more specific measures, such as the status of temporary work. Second, he proposed the creation of a statute for European companies which would include the participation of workers' representatives and, third, the extension to all workers of the right to lifelong education in a changing society. He emphasised that social dialogue and collective bargaining were essential pillars of democratic societies and social progress.

At the Strasbourg European Council in December 1989, 11 Member States adopted the Community Charter of the Fundamental Social Rights of Workers. Britain, alone, did not sign. The Community Charter lists 26 fundamental social rights, ranging from freedom of movement and equal treatment for men and women to trade union rights and rights for the disabled. There are many others, too. Its full title, the Community Charter of the Fundamental Social Rights of Workers, shows its deep commitment to the world of work. In his introduction to the Charter, Jacques Delors wrote that

'it lays down broad principles underlying our European model of labour law [...]. It incorporates a foundation of social rights, which are guaranteed and implemented, in some cases at the level of the Member States or at Community level depending on the field of competence. But it cannot be put into practice without the active participation of the two sides of industry.'

Social Chapter

In the negotiations leading up to the Maastricht Treaty, European trade unions had three priorities. The first was to deepen the competence in social policy of the European Community, and to broaden the range of social issues on which legislation or other instruments could be proposed. The second priority was to extend the scope of issues covered by qualified majority voting and to reduce the option for one Member State to veto a proposal. Third, and most important, was to give force to the role of the social partners in developing, drafting and implementing social policy, especially legally binding framework agreements. Negotiations between the ETUC and the employers' organisations, UNICE and CEEP led to an agreement in October 1991 just before the Maastricht conference. This campaign led to the Social Protocol and Agreement attached to the Maastricht Treaty.

The Social Chapter of the Amsterdam Treaty incorporated the Social Protocol and Agreement, extending social partner rights still further. The Commission must consult the recognised trade union and employer organisations over social policy proposals, at which time the social partners can opt for the negotiation track, leading to a framework agreement. If not, the proposal can go down the legislative route. If proposals go through as directives, the European Parliament also has more influence. Amsterdam gave the Parliament extended co-decision rights with the Council of Ministers on proposals with a qualified majority voting legal base. This includes the majority of social policy questions. In addition, both the Community Charter and the Council of Europe's Social Charter are referred to in the Social Chapter. The Chapter itself was made possible after the Labour Government signed up to both the Community Charter and the Social Protocol, which John Major had opted Britain out of at Maastricht.

The Community Charter and the Social Chapter were not put in place just to please the trade unions or the Social NGOs.

They were seen as crucial steps forward for the European Community as a whole. This is because Europe is not just an economic free trade area. It would never have developed so far and so fast if it had been merely that. The European project has always been based on a historic compromise. Markets have been liberalised and great economic energy has been unleashed. But there has always been an understanding across the European political spectrum, Christian Democrat as well as Social Democrat, that the energy unleashed by these new market forces can have damaging social effects.

And in return therefore, people need protection - rights at work, civil and political rights, citizenship rights, rights for third country nationals, social and economic rights and binding political objectives, or programmatic rights such as the right of people with disabilities to programmes and measures that promote their occupational and social integration. The Joint Campaign document for a new Charter of Fundamental Rights, produced by the ETUC and the Platform of European Social NGOs, does a good job in listing them.

The European bargain over balanced economic and social progress explains why working people in this country are getting more rights at work - from those on working time to parental leave, from equal treatment between women and men to equal rights for part-time workers, from European works councils to equal treatment for workers on fixed term contracts. It has made possible the current negotiations on a European framework agreement on temporary agency work.

Rapid restructuring

Meanwhile, the pace of change has become even more explosive. Under the impact of the single market and the single currency, company mergers and cross-border take-overs have more than trebled. Britain has one of the highest company merger rates of all. Hundreds of firms throughout manufacturing industry and right across the UK and the EU are caught up in the turbulence. So are scores of companies in other sectors, especially banking and finance. It is not just Rover and BMW. That is a glaring example of where an absence of information and consultation rights not only hits workers hard, but also undercuts a government's ability to cope with change as well. The new information and communication technologies and the globalisation of trade and finance are transforming business organisations. The shock waves are hitting workers across the European Union and around the world.

It is worth looking at three policy areas as examples of the need for action:

Information and consultation

It has always been understood that economic integration in the European Community would result in economic and social restructuring - the single market, the single currency, enlargement. The key issue was: how to manage the process of change? What information and consultation rights should workers and trade union representatives have? The first oil shock in 1973/4 and the following recession led to a deep round of company restructuring and rising unemployment. Three directives were adopted to safeguard workers' rights. These were: the Collective Redundancies Directive, the Transfer of Undertakings ('Acquired rights') Directive and the Insolvency Directive. Updated, this legislation continues to underwrite workers' protection today.

As the single market and the single currency, in particular, have increased rapidly the rate of company mergers and take-overs, the three directives have played an important role in protecting workers during restructuring, liberalisation and privatisation, especially in public sector sub-contracting. The 1989 Community Social Charter, as already mentioned, included a set of important clauses on information, consultation and participation for workers, but the Charter was not legally binding. Under the Social Chapter, however, the EU is given the power to bring forward measures on information and consultation and on co-determination.

The European Works Councils (EWC) Directive introduced new rights to information and consultation for workers in transnational European companies. We are still waiting for the draft directive on workers' involvement in a European Company (the European Company Statute), the directive on information and consultation rights for workers in national level companies and the Observatory on Industrial Change. So far what we have is not enough to provide workers with real protection during company restructuring. This has been the direct experience of workers involved in company restructuring throughout many sectors, from the famous case of the closure of the Renault Vilvoorde, in Belgium, onwards. Renault announced the closure of the plant, which was in the constituency of the Belgian Prime Minister, without proper consultation of the Belgian trade unions or government.

The ETUC and Platform of Social NGOs' Campaign for fundamental rights is pressing for all the existing and proposed measures to be bound together into a coherent package. They should be anchored to a right to information and consultation written into the Treaty through the Charter of Fundamental Rights.

The right to strike

The 1989 Community Social Charter specifically lists the right to strike:

> 'The right to resort to collective action in the event of a conflict of interests shall include the right to strike, subject to the obligations arising under national regulations and collective agreements.'

On the other hand, the Social Chapter in Article 137 (6) TEC specifically excludes 'pay, the right of association, the right to strike or the right to impose lock-outs' from the competence of the European Union. This is unsatisfactory, to say the least. If we look at the economic reality we live and work in we can see that economic integration means that the EU is operating increasingly as one economy. Companies are operating increasingly as European companies. There is free movement of capital. There is also free movement of goods and there is meant to be free movement of workers. In December 1998 the Council adopted a regulation on the functioning of the internal market in relation to the free movement of goods among Member States. The regulation requires Member States to take all necessary and proportionate actions to remove serious obstacles to the free movement of goods and to inform the Commission what action it is taking. The regulation explicitly stated that it could not be interpreted as affecting in any way the exercise of fundamental rights as recognised in Member States, including the right or freedom to strike.

The background to the measure is very important. The Commission took action in the context of the truck drivers' strikes in France, which were blockading the movement of goods within and through France to surrounding countries. But the strikes were about the lack of action over working time measures that should have been adopted at the European level. Transport workers had been excluded from the Working Time Directive and yet the road transport sector had already been liberalised from July 1998. In France, liberalisation was resulting in a rush to the bottom in working conditions, as haulage companies became engaged in ever more fierce competition. Drivers were being pressured to work excessively long hours; often they were not being paid for waiting or unloading time.

The absence of common minimum standards in the midst of an intensifying and liberalising European single market in transport led inevitably to strike action which was widely supported by transport workers in other EU countries. The free movement of goods became blocked, not just in France but in the surrounding countries. The right to strike became a central issue for the Council of Ministers as they tried to deal with the situation. The particular issues have not been resolved, and will not be until all transport workers are covered by common rules on working time. Similarly, the wider issue of the right to strike and to take collective action must be faced squarely. It will not be resolved until these rights, including the question of cross-border actions, are anchored in the Treaty.

Collective bargaining

The Community Social Charter included the right to negotiate and conclude collective agreements under the conditions laid down by national legislation and practice. It also included social dialogue at European level, resulting in contractual relations at inter-occupational and sectoral level. The Social Chapter, in Articles 138, 139 TEC, provides for social dialogue at Community level leading to contractual relations and to both framework and voluntary agreements between the recognised trade union and employer organisations.

These Articles were referred to by the European Court of Justice in the Albany Case. Albany, a Dutch textile company, complained that mandatory affiliation to a pension fund system established by collective agreement violated European competition rules. The European Court of Justice emphasised the social policy objectives of the EU, saying that they must be given equal weight to competition policy objectives. The Court said this view was supported by the Social Chapter in Articles 138, 139 TEC, which explicitly support social dialogue and collective bargaining between workers and employers, including at EU level. It is unlikely that these questions have been finally resolved. There are likely to be more cases coming through of a similar nature. As in the examples of information and consultation and the right to strike, an article on collective bargaining in a legally binding Charter would provide greater legal clarity and enhance workers' rights in the European Union.

New Social Agenda

The fact that the European economy is picking up steam, with growth rates increasing and unemployment falling, means that we have a wider window of opportunity to make progress on the Social Agenda as well. We look forward to the French Government's proposals, based on the Commission's Communication, *Towards a New Social Policy Agenda*, to be developed during their Presidency and adopted at the Nice European Council. To run from 2000 -2005, the Commission's Social Policy Agenda places new and pending proposals in the context established by the March Lisbon European Council on jobs, economic reform and social cohesion.

The Lisbon Summit agreed a new strategic goal for the EU over the next decade: to

'become the most competitive and dynamic knowledge-based economy capable of sustainable economic growth with more and better jobs and greater social cohesion'.

The guiding principle of the Agenda will be 'to strengthen the role of social policy as a productive factor'. The communication stresses that social policy has enabled the EU to manage structural change whilst minimising negative social consequences. For the future, modernising the European social model and investing in people will be crucial to retain the European social values of solidarity and justice while improving economic performance.

The core of recent Social Action Programmes has been employment. What is stressed in the Agenda is the Lisbon objective of raising the employment rate, the employment potential, especially among women and specifically in the service sectors. It highlights the IT skills shortage, which is increasing in the EU. Investing in people and life-long learning, objectives agreed in Lisbon, are central. A key challenge is to move from tackling social exclusion to mainstreaming social inclusion into all policy making. Unemployment is seen as the single most important reason for poverty, although, as the UK case shows, poverty can be widespread even where employment rates are higher than the EU average.

The list of specific proposals reveals a major role for the social partners. Under the section on more and better jobs, the social partners will be involved in developing dialogue and negotiations at all levels on lifelong learning, and in developing European common objectives as a reference for social partner action at national level through the employment guidelines. In the area of anticipating and managing change the Commission will consult the social partners on modernising employment relations; follow-up the negotiations on temporary work; consult the social partners on the need to establish, at European level, voluntary mechanisms on mediation, arbitration and conciliation for conflict resolution. The social partners will also be involved with the communication and conference on corporate social responsibility; the communication and action plan on financial participation of workers; the communication on a Community strategy on health and safety and the codification of legislation on working time and health and safety.

In relation to exploiting the opportunities of the knowledge-based economy the social partners will be invited to focus their discussions on lifelong learning and new forms of work related to information technology. As a means of promoting mobility the social partners will discuss an instrument on transferability of pensions within the Pensions Forum. Trade unions and employers' organisations will also be consulted on data protection. Promoting quality in industrial relations will be another focus of the new Social Policy Agenda with the establishment of a reflection group on the future of industrial relations; consultation of the social partners on areas of common interest in collective bargaining and a conference of social partners on the functioning of the social dialogue. In addition to these specific references, the social partners will be consulted on many of the other actions listed under mobility, promoting social inclusion, social protection, gender equality and fundamental rights.

Charter of Fundamental Rights - Nice European Council

Aware of the many effects of rapid economic and social change in the European Union and with enlargement not far away, the Cologne European Council in June 1999 decided that a Charter of Fundamental Rights should be drawn up. It would need to fit in with the next revision of the Treaty, which is to be concluded by the Nice Intergovernmental Conference in December 2000.

The Convention of European and national parliamentarians, and government representatives has been drawing up a draft Charter. The draft should be put to a special European Council in Biarritz in October. In any event, it will go to the Nice Summit in December, under the French Presidency. What the Cologne Summit did not say was just how the Charter should be aligned with the Treaty. Would it be a simple proclamation of fundamental rights or would it be made legally binding through incorporation into the Treaty itself?

The TUC is pleased to see that the CBI supports a Charter that sets out the fundamental values that all Member States share. But we do not accept their argument that, in supporting a legally binding Charter, the trade unions are trying to get in the back door. Like the ETUC, the TUC much prefers to enter through the front door. The Social Charter and the Social Chapter both came in through the front door. The UK Government's approach, which Lord Goldsmith, the UK representative on the Convention has expounded, is to call for a two part document. The first part would list existing rights while the second part would point to where they can be found, in which instrument and how they are enforced. There would not be any new rights and the Charter would not be put into the Treaty.

The TUC wrote to the Prime Minister, explaining why we prefer the Joint ETUC-Platform approach of incorporating the Charter in the Treaty. Put simply, we want to see European citizens gain greater confidence in the European Union and for them to give it greater support. The Cologne Council had this as an objective, too. We are not against aspirational documents. But in our view European citizens are more likely to gain greater confidence if they can see that their rights are legally underpinned in the clearest possible manner.

A good example of this was the inclusion of Article 13 TEC, the anti-discrimination clause in the Amsterdam Treaty. It boosted the confidence of all those European citizens who do face discrimination in their daily lives. Moreover, its relevance is underscored by the inclusion of a far right, racist party in the Austrian Government. A Charter of Fundamental Rights, incorporated in the Treaty, would show European citizens that real progress was being made towards a people's Europe.

Conclusion

The European social bargain is based on a sophisticated balancing act between three sets of values: competition, co-operation and solidarity. This has been the case ever since the European Coal and Steel Community was set up as a forerunner to the European Community. The Treaties carry the values through, providing a legal basis for action. However, the question that is central to the Charter and whether it should be legally binding is: have we still got the balance between economic and social policy right?

Take the example of the single market. A huge legislative programme, based on the Treaty, was put in place to implement the single market. Over 1,400 pieces of legislation have been adopted. But of these only about 100, or around 7% of the total, were in the social policy area. The overwhelming bulk of the legislative programme has been commercial or technical. This reveals a very different picture from the argument put by business groups that they are being weighed down by a mass of social legislation. Most of the legislation they are dealing with is technical or commercial in nature. The argument about whether there is too much 'gold-plating' is important but that is a separate one.

In recent years, important advances have been made in recognising the importance of fundamental rights within the European Union. The Amsterdam Treaty, in Article 6, stipulates that

'[t]he Union shall respect fundamental rights, as guaranteed by the European Convention for the Protection of Human Rights and Fundamental Freedoms signed in Rome on 4 November 1950 and as they result from the constitutional traditions common to Member States, as principles of Community law'.

In addition, as mentioned above, Article 13 of the Treaty introduced requirements relating to non-discrimination and references to the Community Charter and the Council of Europe Social Charter were included in the Social Chapter. Also there is a recognition of European citizenship and the provision of rights such as freedom of movement, the right to vote in local and European elections and the right to petition. The Social Chapter also grants the Union competence to put in place programmes to fight poverty and to promote social inclusion.

In spite of this progress, the process of European integration, with its implications for human rights, requires that real and effective protection of fundamental rights are afforded to the citizens and workers of Europe. These rights need to be set out clearly in one coherent text. Fundamental rights are an indispensable part both in strengthening the social dimension of the European Union and in safeguarding and developing the European social model. Human rights are indivisible. The full set of rights: civil, political, economic, social, cultural and trade union, should be incorporated into the Treaty in a binding manner. An EU Charter of Fundamental Rights, which limits itself to a solemn political declaration, would fall short of what is needed now in terms of the objectives of European construction, the enlargement of the Union and the EU's global role. More importantly, we need to reinforce the faith of European citizens in the European social bargain wherein equal importance is given to social as well as economic progress and within that a focus on individual rights.

Chapter 13

A Clarion Voice For Human Rights

Giampiero Alhadeff and Suzanne Sumner

This chapter analyses the draft Charter by reference to the ideal of a comprehensive Charter at European level proclaiming the indivisibility of civil, political, economic, social, cultural and trade union rights social NGOs have long campaigned for. Such a text is considered necessary to remedy the lack of support and legitimation of the process of European integration which has resulted from too great an emphasis on the economic and monetary aspects. Whereas the draft is praised for its innovative structure which is based on the indivisibility of fundamental rights, it is criticised for its emphasis on economic rights to the detriment of social rights which are, however, recognised and protected in other international conventions. In addition to the weak provisions regarding enforceability of social rights, this is argued to present a regressive step. A more comprehensive EU Charter - enforceable by judicial as well as other mechanisms - has, however, the potential to play a crucial part in the enhancement of universal fundamental rights at European level and indeed the modernisation of social protection and the improvement of economic performance.

Conscious that Europeans were losing heart with the EU project, Viktor Klima, the Austrian Chancellor, in concluding his term as President of the EU, asked that Europe become a 'Clarion voice for Human Rights.' Support for the process of European integration had been undermined by too great an emphasis on the single currency and single market to the detriment of the social dimension of the European Union. The apathy and lack of trust in the Union was never more apparent than in the massive abstention from the polls during the European elections in June 1999.

Trade unions and social NGOs decided to work together for a comprehensive Charter proclaiming the indivisibility of civil, political, economic, social, cultural and trade union rights, which would also specify the rights of citizens and of third-country nationals. The socialist and social democratic majority on the EU Council wishing to tilt the balance of trust, proposed and agreed to draft a Charter of Fundamental Rights, arguing that such a Charter would be a vital opportunity to show the relevance of the European project to citizens.

In July 2000 the executive of the inter-parliamentary and governmental body charged with the writing of the Charter of Fundamental Rights produced the first complete draft. Far from being a comprehensive text, this Charter, if it were to be adopted in its current form, would be a veritable step backwards in human rights provisions. Now, in the final months before the whole issue is to be resolved at the Nice Summit, NGOs and Trade Unions are united in their campaign to ensure that substantial changes are made so that a forward-thinking text may be adopted in time for the December 2000 EU Summit.

How it all began

In 1996, a *Comité des Sages*, chaired by the former Portuguese Prime Minister, Maria de Lourdes de Pintasilgo, and which included Shirley Williams, argued that a base of fundamental rights should be included in the Amsterdam Treaty, but, with little support from Member States, the proposal fell through. The European Commission kept the flame burning by holding national conferences across the Union and by commissioning a further report from another group of legal experts led by Professor Simitis, and the issue was kept alive through the alliance that built up between the Platform of European Social NGOs and the European Trade Union Confederation (ETUC) which organised constant lobbying at the national and European level.

The breakthrough came in 1999 when Gerhard Schroeder, after becoming Chancellor of Germany, wrote to the NGOs and the trade unions, to say that positive action needed to be taken to make the Union more relevant to EU citizens. He proposed to make the Charter of Fundamental Rights one of the key outcomes of the German EU Presidency. It seemed a bold challenge, likely to be turned down once again by most Member States, but the German Presidency played a skilful hand and won a compromise at the Cologne Summit.

EU leaders specified the reasoning behind the development of the Charter but left many questions unanswered, most importantly they left undecided what the final legal status of the Charter would be. They also agreed that they would decide at the end of the process whether the Charter would be a political declaration, a fine set of words with little legal strength or be integrated into the Union Treaties.

In October of the same year, in Tampere, the EU Council took a bold and innovative step to set up a unique body, which eventually called itself the Convention. The new assembly was to be a combination of government representatives, European Parliamentarians, national Parliamentarians and one representative from the European Commission. Once again the German Government played a strong role by nominating Roman Herzog, their former President, to the Convention. His subsequent election to be President of the body heightened the political impact and importance of the assembly and of the document they are charged to produce. Any hopes of some Member States that the Convention and the Charter would be a low-key affair were dashed.

The draft Charter - economic but not social

The Convention sat through the end of 1999 into the year 2000, receiving comments, hearing evidence, debating legal points and trying to make sense of the task in front of them. The ETUC and the Social Platform made representations both written and verbal and mounted seminars and conferences across the EU. In July 2000 the Praesidium of the Convention released its first complete proposal for the Charter.

Refreshingly the draft makes a positive step towards proclaiming the indivisibility of rights. The fifty-two articles of the new draft (CONVENT 45) are separated into 7 sections headed 'Dignity', 'Freedoms', 'Equality', 'Solidarity', 'Citizenship', 'Justice' and 'General Provisions' and are preceded by a Preamble setting the tone of the text. The structure of the Charter must be welcomed for the new and innovative way in which the rights have been divided. Human rights activists have long campaigned for the end to the division between economic, social and cultural rights on the one hand and civil and political rights on the other, a division that did little to promote the indivisibility and universality of rights and served only as an impasse to the legal status of economic and social rights.

The draft should also be welcomed for its clear and comprehensive inclusion of many important rights: the emphasis on human dignity and the unambiguous prohibition on the death penalty and trafficking in human beings, to name a few.

However, despite the extensive volume of contributions and lengthy debate, the draft in the final analysis is a great disappointment. The economic emphasis of the European Union is underlined in the bold confirmation of the freedom to conduct a business and the right to property, including intellectual property, which are stated without being subject to any limitations on the grounds of social responsibility.

However, social rights are written in vague or ambiguous language and subject to additional references to the authority of national laws and practices.

The tone and language of the Charter also stands in stark contrast to many of the recent Communications and Reports from the European Commission and Parliament. At the March 2000 Lisbon Summit, the EU Council underlined the importance of social rights to the future economic strength of the Union, a theme which was then taken up by the Commission's *Social Policy Agenda* published in June of the same year. Social rights and the rights of workers and their organisations are not given adequate importance in this version of the Charter.

The Social Platform and the ETUC have united to reject the Praesidium's draft. They are arguing that the Convention must put right the draft by including the rights which are missing, making good those which would constitute a step backwards and those which are articulated in an ambiguous manner.

Deficiencies, regressions and ambiguities

The Cologne Summit conclusions state that the Charter

'should contain the fundamental rights and freedoms as well as basic procedural rights guaranteed by the European Convention of Human Rights (Council of Europe 1950) and derived from the constitutional traditions common to the Member States, as general principles of Community law.' It should 'take account [...] of economic and social rights as contained in the European Social Charter and the Community Charter of the Fundamental Social Rights of Workers (Article 136 TEC)[...].'

This term of reference for the Convention has been read so as to exclude the creation of wholly new rights, although at no point in the text is it stated that the cited documents should be the only source of orientation.

In creating a new human rights text, one must also look to the documents of the United Nations, the International Labour Organisation and other texts from the Council of Europe, bearing in mind, of course, that most have been ratified by all the 15 Member States. In particular, reference must be made to the Universal Declaration of Human Rights, to the International Covenant on Civil and Political Rights (ICCPR 1966), the International Covenant on Economic, Social and Cultural Rights (ICESCR 1966), the various issue-based instruments of the United Nations such as the Convention on the Rights of the Child (1989), the Convention on the Elimination of all forms of Discrimination against Women (1979), the International Labour Organisation's Declaration of Fundamental Rights at Work (1998) and the Geneva Conventions and their Protocols.

Concerning Social Rights, reference should also be made to the Revised European Social Charter (Council of Europe 1996). Although this Charter has to date only been ratified by France, Italy and Sweden, and therefore cannot be seen to legally bind the other States, it is a far-reaching text that must be ratified by the remaining 12 Member States at the earliest opportunity and should therefore be referred to.

It is surprising to see that, not only is there a failure to cite these key instruments at any relevant point, but the provisions in the Charter take a step back from already agreed principles that Member States have signed up to in other international arenas.

What is missing?

The deficiencies in the draft are substantial and range from the lack of acknowledgement of the right of association, negotiation and collective action at the European level, to the absence of a specific article on equality between men and women. These are recognised in other human rights instruments and their absence from this Charter constitutes serious omissions.

Other rights missing include the right to choose one's occupation, the right to a decent minimum income to ensure health and well-being, the right to protection against poverty and social exclusion, the right to decent housing, and the right to life-long learning. Discrimination on the grounds of nationality is also absent among the grounds of prohibition of discrimination.

Steps backwards

Many social rights, including the right of workers to information, the right to collective action, the right to social security and to health are subject to a subsidiarity clause. In every case, national laws and practices are quoted as limiting these rights. This appears strange, as the right to intellectual property and the freedom to conduct a business are free from any such limitations and Article 50 of the Charter already includes a subsidiarity clause applicable to the Charter as a whole.

It is also regrettable that the Charter does not include a clause of *non-regression* in relation to rights recognised at national level, in such a way as to ensure that this Charter cannot be used to justify a step backwards as regards these rights. Such an article should refer to the Revised European Social Charter, the Community Charter of Workers Fundamental Social Rights, the Declaration on Fundamental Principles and Rights at Work (ILO, 1998), the Convention on the Elimination of All Forms of Discrimination Against Women (UN, 1979), the Convention on the Rights of the Child (UN, 1989).

Ambiguities

There is certainly an issue with the language of the Charter, not only is it sexist, referring constantly to 'he' and 'his', but at certain points in the text the references are not clear and words need to be inserted or concepts explained. For example, the Preamble guarantees 'the rights and freedoms set out hereafter are guaranteed to each person'. Does this guarantee include third-country nationals whether legally resident or not?

The Freedom of research, Right to intellectual property and Freedom to conduct a business should include explicit reference to the public interest, the respect of dignity and, for businesses, a reference to social responsibility.

Article 29 (now 31) should refer to the rights to health and safety protection in the workplace (as does the Treaty of the European Community). Article 43(2) (now 45(2))provides that 'Freedom of movement may be granted to [...] third country nationals'. The word 'may' in this context is, to say the least, ambiguous.

The formulation of Articles 32 (now 34) (Social security and social assistance) and 34 (now 36) (Access to services of general economic interest) is also too open to interpretation. Instead of setting out that, 'Everyone has access to [...]' like, for example, Article 33 (now 35) (Healthcare), these two Articles state, 'The Union recognises and respects the entitlement to [...]' (Art. 32 (now 34)) or, 'The Union respects the access to [...]'(Art. 34 (now 36)). This terminology is unclear and inadequate.

The social rights debate

The root of the criticism of the current draft text is that it evaded the question of social rights and of their enforceability. The issue of enforceability of economic and social rights had been the main point of argument both for civil society and for the Convention. Some Member States, including the UK, wished to exclude these rights entirely. The argument is that many of these rights are programmatic and depend on spending and political programmes for their implementation. Difficult to enforce, social rights end up being seen as 'wish lists' carrying little weight.

This position contradicts the current climate of human rights thinking, which clearly states that all rights are universal and indivisible. Enforcing economic and social rights simply requires a different approach. This often means the division of the rights into what are core rights and those which are objectives to work towards.

Human rights lawyers and experts working on the issue of enforceability of economic and social rights have come up with possible solutions. The UN Committee on Economic, Social and Cultural Rights has tackled this issue in some of their General Comments[1] and elaborated that within each right there is a minimum standard that must be met and can therefore be enforced. They categorised a right into four levels: to respect the right, meaning that they must not be interfered with, to protect it, to ensure it and finally to promote it. These so-called *Limburg Principles* also expanded on the clarification of these rights and analysed how the ICESCR (UN 1966) can be implemented. They carefully detailed the manner in which these rights can be enforced and what would be seen as a breach.[2]

The Platform of European Social NGOs and the European Trade Union Confederation in their joint document made a specific proposal which builds on this work. They maintained that some rights such as the right to equal treatment irrespective of gender, race, social or ethnic origin, religion or belief, disability, age, or sexual orientation should be guaranteed across the territory of the Union and enforced through national courts. But those social rights, such as the right to life-long learning or the right to decent housing, to a decent pension or the right to work, depend for their implementation on political programmes and require policies and measures to ensure that all citizens have access to them. They should therefore be considered as binding political objectives and require more subtle instruments of enforcement.

The novelty of the ETUC–Platform proposal is that it suggests that the European Council, after consultation with the other EU Institutions and civil society, should approve a rolling five-year plan to include targets and enforcement mechanisms for the implementation of these rights. The inclusion of these rights in the Commission's *Social Policy Agenda* would be an ideal mechanism for this programmatic implementation.

A historical opportunity...

The EU Charter of Fundamental Rights, if it incorporated economic and social rights in a manner that was of equal value to civil and political rights and in a way that, even at the most basic levels of respect and protection, could be taken before a legal body, would represent a momentous development in human rights protection. This is a unique opportunity for the EU to take a leading step and is an opportunity that should not be overlooked.

The inclusion of far-reaching social rights, linked in implementation to the *Social Policy Agenda*, would be recognition that the European social protection models are the core of our societies and a major factor of our success in the global marketplace. It would also represent an acknowledgement that we must modernise our social models if we are to use our full potential and improve our economic and trade performance. However, any attempt to modernise social protection will fail if it is perceived as weakening access to rights and protection. Within this perspective an enforceable Charter of Fundamental Rights, using a relevant provision of economic and social rights, would prove an indispensable tool in both safeguarding and modernising our models of social protection and improving our economic performance.

... or a monumental disaster?

Social NGOs and trade unions will not accept the draft as it stands. They will continue to campaign up to the Council meeting in Biarritz in October and will insist that after Biarritz the document is given back to the Convention, along with the comments of the Council, so that it can be improved before the Nice Council Summit. If substantial changes have not been made by this time to address the key deficiencies and pitfalls identified then civil society will join together to insist that this Charter is not accepted.

The issue of legal status is still unclear. Previously we would have argued for the text to be legally binding, and this is still our aim. However, the most crucial issue at present is to get the text right. The Charter is a glorious opportunity for the European Union to become a clarion voice for the proclamation and advancement of human rights. Will it be up to the challenge?

Postscript

Since the writing of this article, important changes have happened in the framing of the EU Charter of Fundamental Rights. On 13 and 14 October, the new draft of the Charter was presented to the European Council at the Summit in Biarritz. The new version, agreed by the Convention and handed over to the French Presidency prior to the Summit, is much improved. Many of the suggestions included in this article and requested by NGOs, Trade Unions and many politicians have been taken on board. It now mentions a right to strike, there is a clause concerning discrimination on the grounds of gender that covers all areas and not just work, social security entitlements are extended to all those legally residing within the EU and not just to workers.

The new Charter is stronger in relation to social rights in that it also refers to the Council of Europe's Social Charter. Most observers agree that it could be stronger - there are still gaps and there remains room for improvement - but that it is an important step in the right direction. It is also true that the process of drafting the Charter has been both unique and historical. Never before has the EU met in such a forum comprising national parliaments, the European Parliament and government representatives and never before have representatives from right across the political spectrum managed to agree and adopt a text solely through negotiation and compromise - never once raising a hand to vote.

The key to the future is whether this is going to become a living Charter. Article 52 gives us a key for future improvements. There will continue to be controversy about whether the Charter should be immediately binding or not. In some ways it would be preferable to wait before making it binding and to give civil society the opportunity to start a major public debate on the Charter. What could be done in Nice is to ensure a reference to the Charter is included in Article 6 of the Treaty. Following this, SOLIDAR recommends that a process is then established to look closely at the legal implications of the Charter and how it is going to work with the European Convention on Human Rights and to set up a procedure by which improvements to the Charter can be incorporated.

The process of a Bill of Rights for Europe is still in the dawning phase, there is much work to be done and NGOs and trade unions must unite behind it to ensure that the voices of the citizens of Europe are heard. Civil society organisations must continue to work on the Charter until it becomes a legally binding part of the European Treaties.

Notes

[1] Committee on Economic, Social and Cultural Rights, General Comments 1-3

[2] The Limburg Principles on the Implementation of the Covenant on Economic, Social and Cultural Rights' Human Rights Quarterly 9 (1987). pp.122-135.

Chapter 14

The EU Charter – A Missed Opportunity to Respond to Citizens' Concerns

Tony Venables

Drawing on empirical evidence, this chapter analyses the level of rights protection Europeans citizens currently enjoy and concludes that peoples' existing rights under EU law are not adequately enforced. An EU Charter of Fundamental Rights is therefore viewed with some scepticism – unless it will be enforceable and thus have real practical effects for citizens. Given the controversies and uncertainties about the Charter's purpose and status, the drafting process is seen as too ambiguous and unbalanced to respond to the questions the general public has about European rights. Focusing on freedom of movement and citizenship, it is argued that information and awareness of these rights is still insufficient, partially as a result of the unclear scope and limits of EU competence which is often shared with Member States' powers. The draft Charter does nothing to clarify or develop these concepts into genuine fundamental rights with effective enforcement mechanisms and remedies. It is also characterised as a missed opportunity in the area of justice to respond to more modern concerns, especially regarding cross-border situations.

The main purpose of this chapter is to examine to what extent the Charter of Fundamental Rights will meet peoples' expectations trying to exercise their rights and responsibilities in a European context. Since 1 January 1993, the organisation to which I belong, ECAS, has run a hotline on visible and hidden barriers to the free movement of people and has also managed for the European Commission a signpost service on European rights. This service composed of ECAS and a multilingual team of 20 lawyers has dealt with 30,000 questions. This represents the single largest database of comparative evidence of how well Europe works or does not. The team has produced a number of reports on cross-border recognition of qualifications, social security, residence rights and consumer transactions. Based on 6000 questions, the service has also done a report on 'how to defend one's rights'.

From the basis of our own experience of dealing with citizens, how do we see the Charter? I would say with some scepticism, because we have not so far detected any substantial demand for such a charter. What we do detect is a widespread malaise about the enforcement of those rights which already exist. It is difficult to judge the mood of the public in such a sensitive area, and perceptions are of course very variable. My guess, however, is that EU leaders, if they do agree a Charter at the end of this year in Nice, will have some difficulty 'selling' the initiative to the public, unless the charter is enforceable and can be shown to have some practical benefits. There is very little discussion, except in EU-watching journals, about the Charter, by comparison with say the much more tangible issue of the passage of the Human Rights Act through the UK Parliament. The attempt by some governments and members of the Convention to 'fell' the idea of a clear but purely declaratory statement of existing European rights as an initiative which could make the EU more popular and visible might receive support, but it will be counterproductive for those people who look to the EU to enforce rights more effectively.

It is important to point out that the Convention set up to create the Charter was not asked specifically to respond to public concerns about European rights. There is a concern about the visibility of rights, and to strengthen the human rights dimension of the EU. But there is also a strong current among members of the Convention and some of the interests gathered round the process which sees the Charter as the beginning of a constitutional process for Europe. Therefore, it is perhaps unfair to look to the Charter in too pragmatic a way.

Despite the ambiguity about the purpose of the whole exercise and the nature of the final text - whether declaratory or enforceable - there are a number of points where the Convention could have done more - and still could - to respond to the questions which all those directly dealing with the public about European rights know exist.

Where can I find information about European rights?

We would like to see in the Charter a clause which states that everyone should have easy access to information about their European rights. As a result of the proposals by the Ombudsman, the Convention has written in articles on 'good governance' and that

> 'every person has the right to have his affairs handled impartially, fairly and within a reasonable time by the institutions and bodies of the Union'.

That is fine for those who have found out where to go with their problem, but it presupposes that people have already received some information about their European rights. Eurobarometer opinion surveys show that there is high demand, particularly from young people, for information about their rights to move around Europe, but that the level of actual awareness remains extremely low. Information failures often have serious consequences with people arriving in another EU Member State unaware that before departure they should have acquired the necessary forms and documents to have residence and social security rights, including minimum health cover. There is often a clash between peoples' expectations, which can be exaggerated all too easily, of what European citizenship means, and national administrations' intent on applying the letter and the exceptions rather than the spirit of European law.

What are my European citizenship rights?

The text of the Charter, by bringing together rights scattered across the EU Treaties with those in the Council of Europe Convention on Human Rights, may help to reduce the information deficit. The most difficult task for our legal team has been to try to explain 'subsidiarity' and what is the dividing line between European and national rights. As a result of the generalised confusion, people tend to either grossly overestimate the extent to which they have European rights, or believe that they have none at all. This is not surprising since citizenship of the Union is an extension of being a citizen of a Member State, and does not exist in its own right. There may, perhaps, be some value in the Charter to help illustrate what are the specifically European rights and what are not. It will need, however, a substantial information budget to carry the discussion beyond the narrow confines of meetings in Brussels and conferences for those already involved in European affairs, to help achieve this objective.

Part of the problem in the area of information about European rights comes from the fact that it is very difficult to explain the scope and limits of EU competence. Free movement rights are an uneasy mix of European and national law and practice. It is difficult to explain why certain European issues such as family law are not covered by the EU. There are problems for people to understand why social security and taxation do not fall under the same regime, why certain pensions are exportable, others not. Unfortunately, the Charter so far has done nothing more than summarise and clarify free movement rights. It has not opened the door, so far, to establish a legal basis for genuine free movement or any development of the concept of citizenship of the Union in the Treaty, except in the general phrase that the Charter may bring together common strands of national rights.

There is also a danger that the Charter could add to the confusion about the respective roles of the European Union and the Council of Europe. It will be recalled that in the run-up to the Amsterdam Treaty, a 'reflection group' of government representatives was divided as to whether the EU should draw its own 'bill of rights' or adhere to the Council of Europe Convention. The majority of NGOs, particularly those specialised in the human rights area, have always favoured the first option. It is an option still open, and would, if taken up, help clarify for citizens the roles of the respective Courts.

Who can deal with my European problem?

The Charter is a missed opportunity in the area of justice to respond to more modern concerns. Certainly the text upholds the principle of legal aid and mirrors the principles of the Council of Europe Convention on Human Rights when it comes to the administration of justice and the right to a fair trial. It could still go further and recognise the principle that everyone should be entitled to free legal advice to enforce his or her rights and that alternative dispute mechanisms to going to court should be available. Such mechanisms, as the EU Council of Ministers has recognised, are particularly appropriate in the area of cross-border consumer transactions, and should in our view be extended to other areas. As our report mentioned above points out:

> 'There is a general feeling that a person making a complaint in another Member State does not have the same chances of winning the case against nationals or residents in another country. Questions like 'how can I enforce my rights/

entitlements against someone living in another EU State' are frequent and show that people expect that there be some sort of EC recourse'.

There has, we suspect, been an imbalance in input to the work of the Convention. Among the NGOs which have put forward their views, very few have done so specifically from the viewpoint of citizens' advice. The purpose has been to promote their particular area of policy, and push back the boundaries of EU recognition of rights. Similarly, among the members of the Convention, the tendency has been to examine how rights are defined at a constitutional level and in international instruments.

The following extract from the report on 'how to defend your rights' is a summary of the concerns which we believe those trying to exercise their European rights would expect to see reflected in the Charter.

- The borderline between EC and national or international competences is difficult for citizens to distinguish. Citizens tend to over-estimate their EC law-defined rights. Some assume that EC institutions will intervene for the defence of individual rights even outside the scope of EC law. This is largely due to expectancies raised by the concept of EU citizenship.

- The existing information and advice services for citizens to assert their rights are insufficient in most Member States, and in any case not homogeneous. Available services are often too specialised and lack sufficient resources. Moreover, directories, which make people aware of these services, are either missing, not up-dated regularly or (for those directories that do exist) are not well-promoted to the general public.

- Partly as a result of the above, citizens are confused about how and where to seek redress. National means of redress are over-looked, preferences going to the well-advertised EC institutions. Hierarchical administrative recourse, the normal first step in defending one's rights, tends to be seen as useless or even counter-productive. There are also signs in many countries that information on appeals mechanisms is not as well publicised as it ought to be.

- Lack of awareness is an obstacle to efficient redress-seeking. Other obstacles in the redress-process itself also exist. Judicial redress is not adapted to the situation of most citizens who cannot afford the costs or the lengths of court procedures. These concerns aggravate the reluctance of citizens recently arrived in a host country and therefore still in a precarious situation, as well as of citizens considering cross-border litigation, who are also confronted with cultural and linguistic barriers.

- Access to legal assistance criteria is generally felt to be too restrictive, cutting out the majority of the population, i.e. people with average income. Well enough not to be eligible for public assistance, most people cannot afford the expense of lawyers and court procedures.

- Extra-judicial redress is not equally available in all Member States, nor is it equally visible or popular in countries where the tradition of such redress exists. The vast majority of problems encountered by citizens when exercising their single market rights are, by their nature, the sort of problem one does not consider to go to court about. Therefore, it is necessary to develop extra-judicial means of redress such as conciliation and arbitration, especially in those countries where ombudsman services are not a tradition.

Finally, the Convention appears to have avoided the issue of access to the European Court of Justice. Our report shows that it is difficult for people to grasp the rationale of the current system whereby in order to defend a specifically European right, it is necessary to go to a national court. As a result, many are deterred from even considering this option. This is not to suggest that we would propose opening the European Court of Justice to individuals in an unconditional way. It is important, however, that the concept of European Citizenship should be underpinned by the right, if other means of redress have been refused, of appeal to the European Court of Justice. It is our belief that if the EU were to adhere to the Council of Europe Convention on Human Rights, the result might not necessarily be appeals to the Strasbourg Commission and Court, but a less restrictive attitude on the part of the ECJ in Luxembourg to appeals from citizens and associations.

Chapter 15

Europe For Everyone: The Social Dimension of the EU and the Present Intergovernmental Conference

John Godfrey

This chapter is concerned with social rights and policy at EU level. It looks beyond the EU Charter, which in itself cannot establish new powers or tasks for the EU or modify existing ones, stressing that it needs to work in synergy with the IGC in introducing Treaty changes which would give the EU a general basis for extended action in the area of social justice. While the EC puts great emphasis on its major economic projects which have important implications for European citizens, the EC's social policy is criticised as being too insufficient to balance some of the negative effects particularly for the poorer and more deprived citizens. It is argued that the combating of social exclusion is an EC obligation enshrined in the Treaty objective of 'raising the standard of living' and should thus be better reflected in a more prominent social policy. For this purpose, some practical examples and proposals for specific Treaty provisions are presented. A universal social policy for all citizens, not merely favouring the workforce, is considered highly important - and the Charter could certainly help to achieve this aim.

It is a paradox that the government of the UK places us at the heart of Europe and yet its people, according to the Commission's most recent poll, give less support to the EU than at any time in the last 20 years. It seems that only a quarter of the sample thought that membership of the EU has been beneficial. Our government, among others, aspires to a people's Europe. So far this has amounted mainly to symbols rather than policies that would help ordinary people directly. Of course, the single market does benefit them indirectly. Perhaps if the Union put this right it would become more popular. It would certainly deserve to.

The single currency, and the disciplines of the Economic and Monetary Union, will have major effects on the people of Europe, including those of the UK so long as our referendum does not go the same way as Denmark's. The advantages will, however, be unevenly spread. The relatively rich countries of the EU have always had large differences in income and wealth among their peoples. But inequality has been increasing. In the EU, poverty has risen with the growth in unemployment, even though social security payments are high by world standards. Poverty and unemployment, leading to social exclusion, are worst among the young, the relatively old, women of all ages and members of ethnic minorities. Modernising the policies of the European Community should help to combat social exclusion where, but only where, they need to be European and act in compliance with the principle of subsidiarity.

Can the purposes of the EU be made fair to all, with policies, best fostered at the European level, for all of its people, as consumers and as citizens, particularly the underprivileged?

Since 1989 a group of European non-governmental organisations, starting with European Research Into Consumer Affairs (ERICA), has been working towards a Europe for its citizens, and one that is democratically responsive to them. The aim of the project for an 'Action Programme for the

198

Citizens of Europe' is that the European Union should adopt policies, best fostered at the European level, for all its people, but particularly for the underprivileged. The present social policy is mainly for those classified as being in the workforce. This limitation is not just. It arose because the Social Charter, and the Treaty changes and the policies that sprang from it, were a response to pressure from the 'social partners'. This term is grotesquely misleading. It means the ETUC and UNICE, to the exclusion of the rest of civil society. The Commission discussed whether social policy should be universal rather than limited to people classified as belonging to the workforce. They, unusually, voted on the issue. The argument for a comprehensive policy was very narrowly lost. As a result, social policies not directed to the needs of the workforce are *ultra vires*. Indeed the Commission has had to retreat from initiatives when taken to the European Court.

Some illustrative examples of proposals that could be put into practice promptly, and that offer the maximum benefit at the least possible cost, are:

- The introduction of a common travel card for people with disabilities. This would give people going to another country in the Union the same facilities as those available to a native of that country. A detailed scheme for this was prepared by ERICA on behalf of the EC Commission's Bureau in Favour of Disabled People in 1989. If this card works well, a similar scheme for older people should follow. Some progress is now being made. Next year the EU is to introduce a blue disabled parking badge giving privileges across the whole EU.

- The economic recession and unemployment have increased poverty, and the poor are less healthy as a result of having an inadequate diet. This has been documented by the UK's Department of Health. The Common Agricultural Policy (CAP) and the Common Fisheries Policy, if further reformed with the needs of vulnerable consumers in mind, could produce high quality food at a lower cost than does the present régime, in a way that could be sustained indefinitely. More open access for agricultural produce from Central and Eastern Europe would similarly help the needy to be better fed. Little effort is being put into innovation that could provide cheaper attractive food with adequate quantities of the important nutrients. Modern biology could help, but the market mechanism alone will not fund the appropriate research and development, because the people with the demand are poor. Because of enlargement and new policies at the WTO, change to the CAP is now unavoidable. Nutritional quality and the price to the consumer should be central to its reform. The French Presidency is to make an initiative on nutrition before December. The issue should also be central to the purposes of the project for a European Food Authority, but there are strong counterpressures from industry.

- After BSE, there is broad agreement that the public interest should be dominant in setting standards for food. The EU has taken steps to reform itself. The UK has set up a Food Standards Agency, as have Ireland and France, and a similar body is now an EU priority. The EU could help in the Transatlantic Consumer Dialogue, at OECD and at UN level. The work of the UN's *Codex Alimentarius* remains dominated by the interests of producers rather than the public. Reform would help EU citizens, but also the less well-protected citizens of less prosperous regions of the world.

- Citizens cannot be confident that food supplies will remain reliable as global climate change takes effect, and the poor consumer would suffer most. In anticipation that our climate will become more extreme, more research using appropriate genetic techniques to produce varieties which could cope with these extremes is now urgent. If global warming becomes an acute problem the market mechanism will work; but it will by then be too late for anything close to an optimal response to the problem. Even if the climate does not change much, research that adapts crops and farm animals to harsh conditions will be valuable in those parts of the world already short of food, and that will be shorter still with the increase in world population.

- The information revolution is already a benefit to business, and to appropriately educated and equipped citizens. Many ordinary people and their families, and certainly those now on the margin of social exclusion, may remain outside this information society. At quite a modest cost a European initiative could begin to help the poor of the inner cities, of peripheral and rural areas, including those in Eastern Europe, to join the better informed. This initiative would work to bring useful information, appropriate to the needs of particular people, in plain language and with attractive presentation to all who choose to use it. It would improve the prospects of employment for those involved. The EU could enhance national initiatives to make the information society more widely available, for instance through libraries, health and social centres; and for parents in schools; and using the next generation of interactive television sets. The European Schoolnet is a welcome start at spreading the information revolution.

These examples share the principle that the EU can enhance the best practice among Member States - in the interest of individuals, families and communities - where the main implementation of a policy may well best be made at national or regional level. This may well be particularly helpful at the all-Ireland level. Governments do not need to be alarmed at the prospect of spending too much. Of course, the Council of Ministers would hold the purse strings.

A more stable European Union will more readily solve the problems of the next enlargement towards the East. The applicants to join the EU may not become full members for some time. There will be a risky period before enlargement is complete. Ordinary people in the applicant countries, not able to take full advantage of the new market economy, are suffering from its effects. Employment has fallen, costs have risen and those on fixed incomes now have a lower standard of living.

People have so far been amazingly patient. Current Member States of the EU should offer the applicants a place in designing the social future for a reunited Europe.

Europe can be seen as an experiment, more ambitious than other regional economic groupings have so far been. It could become a more worthy model for regional associations of states beyond Europe. George Soros said to CIVITAS, the world organisation for civil society:

> '[...] the benefits of global capitalism are unevenly distributed. Generally speaking, capital is in a much better position than labour because capital is more mobile than labour.'

He argued that taxation thus shifts from capital and governments to labour. Probably governments are forming regional associations of states in part so as to protect themselves. Civil society and its NGOs are more vulnerable. Without determined measures, the accelerating globalisation of the economy, of manufacturing and of services, may increase unemployment, and reduce the standard of living of the excluded, with severe social consequences. If the EU helped to foster the development of policies for the disadvantaged in each of the world's regional economic groupings, and encourage the international institutions to respond to this challenge, it would not only contribute to the welfare of people, but would also help towards more peaceful international relations.

There is no doubt that combating social exclusion is included in the European Community's tasks as defined in Article 2 of the EC Treaty, in particular that of raising of the standard of living and the quality of life. As such it should find a natural place in the Charter of Fundamental Rights, even if this ends up as a minimalist compendium of the *acquis*. Having policies for everyone may not become legally enforceable, but at the very least it should be permitted in law.

However, this noble task is not reflected in the provisions of the rest of the EC Treaty. It is thus not implemented in the specific tasks and activities of the present Community. The opinion about the European Union that its citizens hold, particularly those who are disadvantaged or excluded, would be more favourable if the task were seen to be tackled more successfully. We therefore propose the following modest amendments to help the High Contracting Parties and the Community to carry out this task, and request that they be adopted at the present Intergovernmental Conference, and then acted on by the institutions with a determination that matches the urgency of the task.

If the EU improves in the opinion of its public, the broader European project will probably succeed. First it must earn wider popularity. A huge step would be to introduce changes at the IGC that make justice in policies legal. It is equally a contribution to the Charter of Fundamental Rights that the Summit meeting in Cologne set in train. Both initiatives should be completed in time for the Nice Summit at the end of 2000. So it is urgent to propose ideas for making the European Community better for everyone as promptly as possible. It would be wise to add this to the Agenda for the IGC. If this fails, the project should be part of the process of reform foreshadowed by the recent embryonic Franco-German proposals that might lead to a European constitution.

The following are suggestions for specific amendments to the Treaty establishing the European Community:

Title XI, Social Policy, Education, Vocational Training and Youth

- Add to ARTICLE 136, 1st paragraph:

'The Community [...] and the combating of exclusion, and the improvement of the quality of life of all citizens and legal residents of the European Union.'

- Add to ARTICLE 137, paragraph 1, the following indent:

'- social measures in the interests of persons caring for other persons, the young, both as individuals and as members of their families, the disabled, and older persons.'

- Inclusion in ARTICLE 149, paragraph 2, of:

'- making the information society more widely available as a means of achieving those aims.'

These small textual changes would enable new potential for social justice to flourish in the EU. Europe needs a unifying theme. Action to secure a just balance of policies for society as a whole could provide such a theme for Europe's future. The capacity of the EU to initiate and implement such policies should be enshrined in the EU Charter of Fundamental Rights, acting in synergy with the IGC. The 'social capital' of the EU would be increased, in the terminology of the World Bank in its current discussion on sustainable development. Better social integration will encourage co-operation at work, and hence the economic growth on which fuller employment depends.

The Charter of Fundamental Rights will be a solemn proclamation, even perhaps a declaration, against discrimination. However, it seems that the Treaty, even after the current IGC, will still have discrimination embedded in its social provisions. The largest group discriminated against may still be people, mainly women, who work, but are not employed, looking after children and other dependants. This fundamental contradiction will probably remain until a subsequent IGC; but perhaps the novel Convention method that produced the Charter will be a model for rectification during the next development of the enlarging EU.

Acknowledgements

I am deeply grateful to Jacques H. J. Bourgeois, professor of law at the College of Europe, Bruges, for his wise and stimulating help, generously given over many years. The *Action Programme for the Citizens of Europe* was started by *ERICA* (European Research Into Consumer Affairs), the *Centre for Human Ecology*, Edinburgh and the *Centre de Droit de la Consommation*, Université de Louvain-La-Neuve. It has had the valuable support of *COFACE* (Confédération des Organisations Familiales de la Communauté Européenne), *EUROLINK AGE*, and *MIDEPH* (Mouvement pour l'Information, les Droits et l'Expression de la Personne Humaine). I am also grateful for the warm welcome given to this collaborative project by the *European Women's Lobby* and *CEG* (Consumers in Europe Group).

Chapter 16

Fear and Loathing in the EU: Ethnic Minorities and Fundamental Rights

Sukhvinder Kaur Stubbs

Reflecting on recent events in Austria and the situation of minorities and migrants all over Europe, this chapter expresses great concern about the increasing tolerance towards far-right agitation and action which stir fears about the alleged threat migrants pose to prevailing notions of society based on outdated models of nation state and sovereignty. A Charter is seen as having real potential to overcome nationalistic and xenophobic attitudes and establish a new cultural and political union across Europe - a community of communities with common interests and values. It needs, for this purpose, to embrace the principles of indivisibility and universality of fundamental rights by enshrining political and civil as well as social rights across all areas of EU policy and law to prevent exclusion, disadvantage and discrimination of minorities and third-country nationals. As a culturally heterogeneous country, the UK is called upon to take a lead in promoting equality and diversity in a human rights framework, thereby also re-conceptualising 'Britishness' in an outward-looking, inclusive society. The Charter, viewed in the context of the emerging European federalism, is seen as a valuable instrument for furthering new models of citizenship transcending national boundaries.

The establishment of the Austrian People's Party-Freedom Party of Austria (ÖVP-FPÖ) coalition in 1999 had one admittedly good effect. It shocked us out of our complacency. We had begun to be lulled into the belief that never again would Fascism gain a foothold in a modern European government. Then along came Jörg Haider, leader of the so-called Freedom Party, who featured on the February cover of both *Time* and *Newsweek* magazines, looking every inch the plausible, modern statesman.

The rise to prominence of Haider, who charmed sections of the Austrian electorate with his remarks in praise of his fellow countryman Adolf Hitler's employment policies, was as dramatic as it was disturbing. Ezer Weizman, the President of Israel pronounced that 'the situation in Austria now is exactly the same as it was in Germany 70 years ago'.

Some 150,000 protestors took to the streets in Vienna, 20,000 demonstrated in Brussels and further thousands gathered across the capitals of Europe. All the members of the EU issued bilateral sanctions against Austria. However, the EC itself was unable to take any action on the grounds that the government was democratically elected. Within weeks, the EU Member States were themselves looking for face-saving ways to end sanctions.

These historic events took place simultaneously with the libel action by historical 'revisionist' writer David Irving against Deborah Lipstadt and her publisher. While most commentators roundly condemned Irving and rejoiced in his defeat, there were, depressingly, the first signs of a 'Holocaust fatigue' as alluded to by David Cesarani, Professor of Modern Jewish History at Southampton, and others. Commentators, such as Brian Sewell, jadedly asserted that 'enough has been made of their Holocaust' and Julie Burchill made some typically intemperate remarks about whingeing Jews. While these could be written off as attention-seeking exercises in political incorrectness, it is perturbing that there were editors and sub-editors who saw no objection to such sentiments seeing the light of day in print.

It should hardly need reiterating but 'Fascism' did not die with the victory of the Allies in 1945. Across Europe, Jews, Muslims, Roma and other people with a black or ethnic minority background continue to face disadvantage, discrimination and racism. In Spain in 1998, the Romany Union case list included 32 instances of racism and discrimination specifically against Gypsies; 40 racist attacks involving abuse by authority or police brutality and 27 specific and documented cases of attacks by violent groups. During the same year, they recorded 15 trials arising out of accusations of racism. The case list also included 85 instances of discrimination in employment and social matters.

The police records for France in the same year report 191 racist incidents, 26 of which were violent and 82 anti-semitic in nature. A recent report canvassing social attitudes among French people showed that up to 40% of the population were prepared to admit openly racist views. In Germany, for the same period, there were 434 offences driven by the far right. Although this represents a small decline from the previous year, the far right there continued to attract more people; in 1998, they brought together 53,000 partisans (an increase of 11% from the previous year) of whom 8,200 are considered extremists ready to use violence and attack foreigners.

More reassuringly, the Finnish Government's investigatory commission published statistics in 1998, which confidently state that there had been no murders or attempted murders motivated by racism or xenophobia. They do, however, list four acts of violence with explosives or firearms which claimed six victims, and ten physical assaults. The police report of the same time showed 194 crimes of a racist nature. Most of the victims of these crimes were of Somali origin.

Clearly then, Europe is still not even a safe or free place for ethnic minorities, let alone equitable, just or fair. Yet when on the 25 March 1957, the King of the Belgians, the Presidents of the Republic of Germany, French Republic and Italian

Republic, the Grand Duchess of Luxembourg and the Queen of the Netherlands came together in Rome to lay the foundations of an even closer union among the peoples of Europe, they must have been, in some part, motivated by the atrocities of the world wars. The desire they expressed in the Treaty of Rome to pool resources to preserve and strengthen peace and liberty is yet to be realised.

In the light of this situation, two immediate questions come to mind:

Firstly, how can it be that, within 60 years of the Holocaust, far-right agitation and action is not only tolerated by the majority ethnic European population but earns a place in government?

Secondly, to what extent will the proposed Charter of Fundamental Human Rights strengthen the ability of the European Union, founded as it is on the principles of liberty, democracy, respect for human rights and fundamental freedoms, to challenge the continuing blight of racism and protect the rights of minorities?

The revival of far-right agitation

Answering the first question requires a closer look at the situation in Austria.

The FPÖ commands some 27% of the vote. A recent report in the Guardian profiles a typical Haider voter.

'These are the new yuppies who are interested in their careers and not in immigrants. [...] They're not really interested in the roots of the Freedom Party. For them, it's the party that takes us very fast into the chic future.'

Such people would not consider themselves or the FPÖ to be racist, and feel somehow disassociated from the legacy of fascism. They consider it to be a democratic party which can be deselected if it fails to deliver.

Yet, many anti-Haider protestors argue that Austria is not yet a true democracy, only a national democracy. The Austrian Platform for a World Against Racism claims that more than 10% of the population is systematically denied all political rights and participation by being kept in the status of 'foreigners'. Even in the trade unions, there are no equal voting rights for all workers and employees. The system guarantees equality not to human beings but to citizens only. The Platform claism that the democratic system imposed on Austria after the Second World War has been compromised by the conservatives, far right and the social democrats. In fact, it is underpinned by a pre-war-style nationalism, with racist segregation and exclusion incorporated into national policy. They believe that this lack of balance in the political system has led to the uprising of a party that is openly promoting a revision of Nazi history, playing on racist sentiments among the populace with political impunity.

Austria is not alone in its extremism. Right-wing parties are flourishing across Europe and many have secured seats in national parliaments - some, for example in France, Switzerland and Italy, receiving over 15% of the vote. In the UK, the National Front has limited influence but the mainstream Conservative Party stands accused of repeatedly playing the race card in issues ranging from asylum to NHS doctors, a policy their central office clearly feels pays political dividends.

It is commonly believed that Austrian racism, like that of many other EU countries, is based on border control - it is about who gets to be in Europe. Austria feels particularly vulnerable. Like Germany, it borders Eastern Europe and the prospect of cheaper migrant workers with their 'non-Christian' values threatens to undermine its notion of society. Haider's vision, set out in his 1995 book 'The Freedom I Mean', clearly articulates this:

'Any policy of immigration must insist on assimilation and adaptation to the culture and norms of the indigenous population. Especially in education we have to defend Christian values [...] 10,400 jobs were created in Austria and all of them were filled by cheap foreign labour [...][Our politicians consider it] more important to experiment with our youth as guinea pigs in abstract, multi-cultural programmes[...]. Our enemies are legion both in eastern Europe and the west, where the threats are more subtle and insidious.'

Islam, it would seem, has taken over from the Soviet Union as the reflex enemy of the west, its baleful influence visible everywhere from book burnings to the brutal theocracy of the Taliban in Afghanistan. In a phenomenon now commonly termed 'Islamophobia', Muslims are perceived as unwilling to adapt to western ways and customs and thereby even reasonable people feel able to attack them with impunity. Clare Hollingsworth, writing in the International Herald Tribune, stated that

'Muslim fundamentalism is fast becoming the chief threat to global peace and security, as well as a cause of national and local disturbance through terrorism. It is akin to the menace posed by Nazism in the 1930s.'

Far from being a global threat levered by the dead hand of an Ayatollah, Islam has as many different faces as Christianity but little protection in law or civil society.

Muslims continue to be the victims of the new Europe. Over a period of 70 years, some 100,000 Muslims are known to have been 'ethnically cleansed' from the north-east region of Greece alone. Across Europe, Muslims are denied the right to dress as they wish - to express themselves freely. They face some of the highest levels of exclusion from the labour market, live in the poorest housing conditions and have little or no representation through civil or political leadership.

Racism has physical and cultural components and victims are often attacked or discriminated against both because of their appearance and a perception that their culture or belief is alien or inferior. Muslims, like Jews, Roma and Gypsies are regarded with fear and loathing in equal measures as the cultural 'Other'. Fuelled by offensive and stereotypical media coverage, such attitudes now prevail in the ostensibly democratic Member States of the European Union. These attitudes are often most despicably manifest in the exclusionary immigration and asylum policies of the Member States.

Even in the UK, the Immigration and Asylum Act of 1999 was reported by Amnesty International as being severely detrimental to refugee rights. Representations were made on the extension of pre-entry controls, the need for effective judicial oversight of the detention of asylum seekers, and the need to ensure access to high quality legal advice if asylum-seekers were dispersed around the UK. The High Court decided in July that the practice of prosecuting and imprisoning those using false travel documents to transit the UK was contrary to international refugee law. In particular, the treatment of unaccompanied refugee children made for a series of recommendations on child asylum seekers.

The efforts to contain asylum seekers appear quite disproportionate to the numbers involved. For example, in 1998, the Office for National Statistics reports 460,000 people migrated to the UK. Of these, 46,000 were asylum seekers, just over 40,000 were young Commonwealth citizens entering on working holiday visas, while returning Britons accounted for 80,000 people. The remainder were job seekers from other EU countries. Certainly the asylum applications for 1999 were higher but this period included the war in Kosovo described by Jamie Shea, the Nato spokesperson as 'the greatest humanitarian disaster since the end of World War Two'.

Compassion alone would be moral enough grounds to adopt a more humanitarian approach to those seeking asylum in Europe. The great irony is, however, that in the coming years the ageing EU population will increasingly depend on immigrant labour. These people will not be a 'burden' but a necessity to our economy. In Germany alone, the old-age dependency ratio is set to rise from 22% to 47% by 2030. Across the OECD countries, it is moving from 19% in 1990 projected to 28% in 2020 and 37% by 2040. Economists detail the need for a new sort of migrant that moves resourcefully back and forth across an EU border usually from Eastern Europe to Germany and Austria, often earning a living in the Union while supporting a family outside it.

But rather than deal intelligently with the issue of immigration, the Member States of the EU continue to buttress themselves and fortify their barriers with rhetoric that keeps nationalism and xenophobia nicely simmering. Member States pursue all the economic benefits of the EU but deeply resist the political consequences. The Union is still a 'Europe of Bankers'. The myriad visions and initiatives designed to transcend this solely monetary goal and establish a solidarity based on a set of common values have, to date, failed.

It is for this reason that the EU Charter of Fundamental Rights is so timely. At the Cologne Summit on 4 June 1999, it was decided that a Charter on Fundamental Rights of the European Union should be drawn up. The European Council stated:

> 'There appears to be a need, at the present stage of the Union's development, to establish a Charter of fundamental rights in order to make their overriding importance and relevance more visible to the Union's citizens.'

The Charter includes the general rights of liberty and equality as well as fundamental rights that pertain to the Union's citizens. It also takes into account economic and social rights. For the European Parliament, the Charter represents one of its constitutional priorities.

Preceding the Charter was the Amsterdam Treaty, which marked a decisive step on the way to an ever clearer recognition of the principle of fundamental rights protected by the European Union. It affirms the Union's commitment to human rights and fundamental freedoms and explicitly confirms the Union's attachment to fundamental social rights. It does this by referring to a number of other charters and conventions including the 1950 European Convention on Human Rights, the 1961 European Social Charter and the 1989 Community Charter. Although the Amsterdam Treaty gives no explicit recognition of particular fundamental rights, it establishes procedures intended to secure their protection. Of particular relevance is Article 13 TEC which empowers the Council to take action against discrimination concerning sex, racial or ethnic origin to discrimination regarding religion, belief, disability, age or sexual orientation.

Certainly, the Amsterdam Treaty consolidates and advances the process of unification and its adoption has given greater urgency to the need for an explicit recognition of fundamental rights. Such rights would extend into the Second (Common Security and Foreign Policy) and Third (Justice and Home Affairs) 'Pillars' of the EU Treaty. Such nationally sensitive areas as freedom, security and justice are currently largely outside the scope of Community law, falling instead within the jurisdiction of individual Member States.

Those who would argue that the EU Charter is unnecessary because the great building blocks of Human Rights already exist within the UN and Council of Europe Treaties fail to acknowledge its real potential. By working across all the three 'Pillars' of the Treaty, fundamental rights could actually override the sovereignty of Member States and so establish a new cultural and political union across Europe, in which the nationalistic and xenophobic mindset that contributes so profoundly to racism would be undermined. In its place could emerge a more inclusive society, transcending existing national boundaries, standing in solidarity against racism and human rights abuses.

Admittedly, the argument is as appealing to politicians as getting the proverbial turkeys to vote for Christmas. National sovereignty remains the mainstay of populist politicians. What is required is that increasingly rare animal in the present mediocre political climate - courage and conviction. Do any leaders have it in them to rise above the short-term dictates of political pragmatism, to persuade their electorates of the hopelessness of the prevailing situation? The structural changes to the labour market in Europe are irrevocable. Globalisation of the economy has its consequences for the external relations of the Community with third countries. A continent of xenophobic nation states is no more tenable than a dubious union maintained as an essentially white fortress with the principle objective of keeping out the hordes of Muslims and former communists threatening from the east. These walls will fall.

The Charter gives credence to the notion of Europe as a community of communities, where social values based on common interests can be forged. A community of communities based not simply on nationalism and economic benefits, but with a conscience aspiring to equality, a soul seated in justice and, at its heart, social inclusion. The Charter of Fundamental Rights affords us the opportunity to build a society across Europe based on rights rather than a jingoistic free market striving for 'Profit über alles'.

The EU Charter: challenging racism and protecting minorities?

There remains though, the second question. Despite any potential ability of the proposed Charter of Fundamental Rights to speed up the process of unification and establish a new social model for Europe, will it actually make any real difference to people with ethnic minority backgrounds?

For ethnic minorities across Europe, there are particular areas of concern relating to the lack of clarity in existing provisions, the indivisibility with social and economic rights and the situation of third-country nationals.

Let us consider first, the importance of clarity. The growing activities and actions undertaken in the European Union framework by different institutions and bodies give to citizens an impression of confusion and contribute to a lack of confidence in European institutions. Our notion of a community of communities, of a Europe of Citizens, remains a vague idea for a large number of people who do not know what it could represent to them. The ethnic minorities most likely to be in need of protection are prone to become particularly disadvantaged especially where they are unfamiliar with mechanisms for redress, may experience communication difficulties and will probably be excluded from mainstream institutions. (For example, how many ethnic minority staff are employed by the European law courts? How many black MEPs are there?) Fundamental rights can only be exercised if people are aware of their existence and conscious of their ability to enforce them. Visibility is vital in permitting individuals to know and to gain access to their fundamental rights. The current system of citations conceals the existence of these rights making them incomprehensible to individuals and violates the principle of transparency.

Next, the issue of indivisibility. As things stand, social and economic rights are not accorded the same status as civil and political rights. Yet, no one has demonstrated any water-tight distinction between social and civil rights. Civil rights, as currently set out, do not adequately protect the socially excluded, and ethnic minorities in particular, from the disadvantages and discrimination they face. We may need to formulate new rights such as the right to resort to collective action. The inclusion of social and employment clauses resonates strongly with ethnic minorities who are often the most vulnerable to the effects of increasing mobility of capital and the shifts in the labour markets.

Aspirations to rights relating to fair remuneration and adequate social security, which might seem reasonable enough, are, however, apparently a source of grave anxiety to one tiny minority in particular - the wealthy industrialists across the Member States of the EU. The CBI in Britain, for example, opposes the Charter fearing, among other things, the possibility of challenges in court to restrictions on the right to strike, union recognition and on worker consultation. They warn that the markets are unable to bear such unprecedented legislation. Yet labour markets have proven hugely flexible in the past and the ability of fundamental rights to undermine them remain limited. When Germany underwent reunification after the collapse of the Berlin Wall, fears were expressed that the next collapse would be that of the German economy, as it absorbed the weaker Eastern sector. Such fears proved ultimately unfounded.

Of particular relevance to these fundamental rights is the social and economic discrimination experienced by the Roma people. It is most severe in Greece and widespread in a number of the applicant countries including Bulgaria, the Czech Republic, Hungary, Romania, Slovakia, and Kosovo with assaults often taking place against a background of vilification of Roma by sections of the media and public. Amnesty International reported that in Slovakia, Roma continued to face ill-treatment at the hands of law enforcement officials, but the authorities failed to carry out prompt, impartial and thorough investigations of ill-treatment. They highlight a pattern of large-scale police operations which appear to target entire Romani communities. At a particular incident in Uehra in December 1999, hundreds of Roma people, including children, were forced out of their homes at 6am by nearly 100 armed police. Their property was damaged, they were allegedly subjected to racial abuse and violence and injured victims were apparently refused treatment.

Finally, the situation of some 17 million third-country nationals, who reside legally in the 15 Member States, provides the greatest scope for improvements to the rights (and indeed, due responsibilities) of ethnic minorities. One significant asset of fundamental rights is the range of their application. It would be inconsistent with the universality of a number of fundamental rights to limit their application to EC citizens only. Third-country nationals, asylum seekers and migrant workers cannot be exempted from the duty to respect fundamental rights. The virtual omission therefore of third-country nationals from current drafts creates some cause for alarm. In fact, third-country nationals are mentioned only twice in Article 15(3) (Freedom to choose an occupation) and Article 45(2) (Freedom of movement and of residence).

Article 15(3) entitles nationals of third-countries who are authorised to reside in the territories of the Member States to working conditions 'equivalent' to (which does not necessarily mean 'equal to') those of citizens of the Union.

Article 45(2) states that

'[f]reedom of movement may be granted, in accordance with the Treaty establishing the European Community, to nationals of third countries legally resident in the territory of a Member State.'

The freedom of movement is not actually granted although the possibility is envisaged. Even if granted in theory, the freedom of movement would be restricted to the right to travel for a period of no more than three months. In practice, third-country nationals would in any case have to wait for the Council to adopt measures setting out the conditions under which they may travel before any such rights could be realised.

It is important to recall that nationals of third-countries have been contributing in an active, indeed fundamental, way to the construction of the European Union for many years. Whole sectors of the economy depend on their contribution, not to mention the role they have played in urban renewal and the enrichment and broadening of social, cultural and artistic life and in the overall development of the Member States where they are resident. Yet, third-country nationals, despite having the same obligations as European Union nationals, are not accorded the same rights.

Currently, third-country nationals, in general, enjoy neither freedom of movement nor the right to settle; under Community law they do not have the right to all social and economic benefits granted by the Member States to their nationals; they do not have the freedom to have access to economic activities in the territory of the European Union. EU nationals may be favoured. Community law does not guarantee them the same conditions for exercising their activities nor guarantee them equal treatment in the area of social protection. Third-country nationals do not enjoy the political rights accorded to European Union nationals - they do not have the right to vote or to stand as a candidate in local or European elections.

This difference in treatment, essentially on the basis of nationality, contradicts the initial intentions of the architects of the Treaty of Rome who included the general principle of non-discrimination on the basis of nationality. Sadly, this principle has subsequently been interpreted as being restricted to the nationality of Member States of the European Union. This also runs counter to the range of international and European instruments for the protection of the rights of the person. One simple solution would be to extend European citizenship to persons residing legally in Member States for at least five years.

With so much to gain for the ethnic minorities across the EU and the accession states, the active resistance from our own government is surprising - especially given the lead role played by the British in the adoption of Article 13 TEC. The British position on the Charter seems grudgingly to accept it as an exercise to give transparency to rights that already exist, but fear it as a backdoor route to a European constitution. Andrew Duff MEP is clear about the Charter becoming a federal constitution. Quoted in the FT Andrew states:

> 'The consequences of the charter installing a fundamental rights regime within the [EU] treaties is part of the federalising process, and I think everyone apart from the Brits seems to be quite clear about that.'

Of all the EU countries, Britain has one of the strongest legislative frameworks against racism. It has much to offer in providing the leadership and example to protect the interests of minorities.

Ironically, the relative achievements of Britain are more a result of a multi-cultural drift, a passive rather than conscious response to ethnicity. Consequently, they can appear as mere lip service only thinly disguising deep-rooted and institutionalised racism within society as all too evidently revealed by the enquiry into the murder of Stephen Lawrence. In the historical absence of any human rights framework, ethnic minority issues are still considered essentially a problem for minorities themselves and serving only the interests of minorities rather than as a challenge for the whole society. Ethnic minorities as part of the British landscape are barely recognised.

Sadly, the prevailing and mythical view of Britain is of a culturally homogeneous land, a spurious impression drawn from a highly selective, collective nostalgia for the way things supposedly were and notions of empire and colonial conquests. Speaking to the Royal Society of St George in 1961, Enoch Powell is quoted as saying:

'Tell us what binds us together; show us the clue that leads through a thousand years: whisper to us the secret of this charmed life of England, that we in our time may know how to hold it fast.'

Later he concluded that the life of nations, like the life of men, is lived largely in the imagination. In reality, Britain has been and continues to be a fractured land, politically and ideologically divided. Mike and Trevor Phillips famously depict the docking of the Windrush not in a unified and culturally distinctive land but one where the ethnic conflicts, debates and disputes predate its arrival by centuries.

The prospect of the Charter has exposed the fragility about our own sense of sovereignty and what it means to be British.

In an attempt to counteract accusations of breaking up the UK through transferring power to the regions and the European Union, the Prime Minister said 'Britishness' today was rooted in shared values of 'fair play, creativity, tolerance and an outward looking approach to the world' adding that it was no longer based on 'territory or blood'. The opportunity exists to use emerging European federalism to redefine what it means to be British. Outmoded nationalist and even liberal (which is to say, laissez-faire) models of citizenship which have dominated the discourse on multi-culturalism need to give way to a plural approach where priority is given neither to unity nor to diversity. The needs of individuals and their communities optimally balanced instead, through inter-cultural deliberation with human rights standards providing the ground rules for negotiations. The Charter of Fundamental Rights, based as it is on measures such as the European Convention on Human Rights now incorporated into UK law, is already extensively debated across diverse faiths, ideologies and cultures. It already anticipates a language of global citizenship. The debate on the EU Charter and a federal constitution can itself be used to set the boundaries for a national self-imaging.

Britain can choose to rest on its laurels, simply pat itself for its existing diversity and complacently press for minor amendments to national and European laws. Underpinning this would be a continuing apathy towards other Member States and a general fear of the world outside. Alternatively, it can blaze a modern trail, promoting the acceptance of equality and diversity as part of a human rights framework and re-conceptualising what it means to be British in an outward-looking, non-nationalistic, progressive ideology. Let's not forget that the motivation for the human rights standards enshrined in the EU Charter of Fundamental Rights follows from the Second World War and the ill treatment of minorities in occupied Europe. As the sinister emergence of Haider reminds us, that spectre is not as far behind us as we would wish to imagine.

Bibliography

Amnesty International, International Report 2000Austrian Platform Against Racism. Press release, 1 February 2000.

Brown, Kevin in: *The Financial Times*, 28 March 2000.

Cesari, David in: *The Guardian.*

Experts Group Report on Fundamental Rights, Affirming Fundamental Rights in the EU - Time to Act (EC, 2000).

EU Charter of Fundamental Rights, European Parliament Resolution (1999/2064COS).

Grant, Linda in: *The Guardian*, 26 August, 2000.

Heffer, Simon. *Like A Roman. The Life Of Enoch Powell.* Phoenix, 1998.

Johnson, Lonnie. 'On the Outside Looking In.' in: Central Europe Review, 27 March 2000.

Parker, Andrew in: *The Financial Times*, 28 March 2000.

Phillips, Mike and Trevor Phillips. *Windrush. The Irresistible Rise of Multi-Racial Britain.* Harper Collins, 1998.

Refugee Council, Inexile. August 2000.

Sierra, Maria Miguel. ENAR press release, August 2000.

Stubbs, Sukhvinder. 'The Hooded Hordes of Prejudice.' in: New Statesman, February 1997.

Versi, Ahmed in: *Muslim News*, 28 July 2000.

Wistrich, Enid and David Smith. 'Ethnic Minority Experience in EU Countries'. Reported in: Runnymede Bulletin, March 2000.

Chapter 17

The Charter of Fundamental Rights and EU Enlargement: Consolidating Democracy or Imposing New Hurdles?

Jackie Gower

This chapter looks at the place of human rights on the enlargement agenda and the reaction in the applicant states to the proposed Charter. As all candidates need to meet international standards of democracy and human rights and will also have to adopt the EU Charter as part of the acquis if it is agreed at Nice, it is suggested that a Charter would help to consolidate democratic structures in Central and Eastern Europe. The applicant states welcome the Charter as a positive development, but have also voiced some criticism, particularly regarding the neglect of minority rights. Having only recently become part of the Council of Europe's common human rights regime, they are also concerned about the risks of the Charter introducing once again different standards and interpretations. It is feared that the controversies about the Charter might cause a deferment of the conclusion of the IGC and hence a set-back to the enlargement timetable.

Introduction

The European Union is currently engaged in accession negotiations with ten of the former communist countries of Central and Eastern Europe[1] plus Cyprus and Malta. Turkey is also officially recognised as an applicant state but has not yet met the criteria for opening negotiations, largely because of deficiencies in its record on human rights. It is widely assumed that the list of potential EU members will grow longer over the next few years as several more of the successor states of both the USSR and the Yugoslav Federation have aspirations to become part of the Union. The prospect of enlargement on such a scale is totally unprecedented in the history of the EU and presents many major challenges for both the applicant states and the Union itself.

Although most attention has been devoted to such practical issues as to how the institutions will function in a Union of nearly thirty states or how the budget can be stretched to pay for the costs of extending the structural funds and Common Agricultural Policy to so many relatively very poor states, there has also been some concern about the need to protect its sense of collective identity and purpose based on shared values and principles. The dramatic events of 1989 spurred the Member States at both Maastricht and Amsterdam to spell out more explicitly in the Treaties what those core values are, and the Copenhagen Council in June 1993 set out the specific criteria by which applicant states would be assessed as to their eligibility for membership. The present endeavour to agree a Charter of Fundamental Rights can therefore be seen as the logical extension of this development, although enlargement is by no means the sole reason for the initiative.[2]

Assuming that the Charter is agreed at Nice, it will become part of the *acquis*[3] that the applicant states will be required to adopt prior to membership, irrespective of whether it is formally incorporated into the Treaty on European Union. Therefore, at a time when the EU is preparing to take in a large number of very new democracies, the adoption of such a Charter would not only strengthen the EU's own democratic foundations, but also help to consolidate the still fragile democratic structures in Central and Eastern Europe. This potential role of the Charter has been widely recognised and welcomed in the applicant states, but there has also been some concern that it might have the effect of erecting new hurdles on their road towards EU membership by imposing new obligations on them. There is also the danger that if the Member States are unable to reach a consensus on the Charter at the Nice Council, the conclusion of the IGC itself may be delayed and hence the enlargement timetable be set back yet gain. This essay will therefore look at the place of human rights on the enlargement agenda and the reaction in the applicant states to the proposed Charter of Fundamental Rights.

Human rights and EU enlargement

It had always been implicitly understood that membership of the European Community was restricted to those states that met international standards of democracy and respect for human rights. Three of the present Member States, Greece, Spain and Portugal, were only able to join once they had returned to the democratic fold, and throughout the Cold War all the countries in the Soviet sphere of influence were automatically excluded. The Treaty on European Union, agreed at Maastricht, introduced a much more explicit reference to respect of fundamental rights as guaranteed under the European Convention for the Protection of Human Rights and Fundamental Freedoms (ECHR) as a general obligation of the Union, and significantly also made reference to respect of fundamental rights 'as they result from the constitutional traditions common to the Member States.'[4] However, it was only in the Amsterdam Treaty that membership was directly linked to respect for fundamental rights, with Article 49 TEU providing that 'any European State which respects the principles set out in Article 6(1) TEU may apply to become a member of the Union.'

Article 6(1) TEU states that

'the Union is founded on the principles of liberty, democracy, respect for human rights and fundamental freedoms, and the rule of law, principles which are common to the Member States.'

For the first time also, a new Article 7 TEU lays down procedures for dealing with 'a serious and persistent breach by a Member State' of those principles, a provision undoubtedly included with a wary eye over the shoulder to the waiting ex-communist states, although it was to be an existing member that first ran into difficulties with it.

This clarification of the membership criteria in the Treaties was undoubtedly a response to the dramatic changes that had taken place in Central and Eastern Europe since the late 1980s. The EC/EU suddenly faced the challenge of a large number of former communist states declaring their intention to apply for membership and clearly expecting that they would be rapidly welcomed into the 'democratic club'. The EU's response was rather cautious, recognising the enormous scale of the political and economic transformations that they were engaged in and the danger that a 'premature' enlargement could undermine the stability of the Union itself. It was decided that criteria needed to be established for judging when an applicant state was 'ready' to begin accession negotiations and to spell out more clearly the membership requirements. Therefore, in June 1993 at the Copenhagen European Council the accession criteria were formally adopted:

'Membership requires that the candidate country has achieved stability of institutions guaranteeing democracy, the rule of law, human rights and respect for and protection of minorities, the existence of a functioning market economy as well as the capacity to cope with competitive pressure and market forces within the Union. Membership presupposes the candidate's ability to take on the obligations of membership including adherence to the aims of political, economic and monetary union.'[5]

These 'Copenhagen criteria' have been used by the Commission as the basis for the preparation of detailed assessments of the situation in each applicant country, both in the production of its initial official 'Opinion' on the application and in the Annual Progress Reports that have been produced since 1998. Although all the criteria are clearly important, the *political* criteria are regarded as the *sine qua non* for beginning accession negotiations. Thus in 1997, when the Commission published its Opinions (known as the *avis*) as part of Agenda 2000, Slovakia was the only one of the ten Central and East European applicants to fail the democracy test and therefore was excluded from the list of 'first wave' states, agreed at the Luxembourg Council in December, despite doing quite well on the economic front. Only after the defeat of Prime Minister Meciar and the election of a government much more committed to democracy was Slovakia able to join the accession negotiations. Turkey remains the only applicant state still excluded from the negotiations and it is its poor record on human rights that is the main obstacle.

Thus it is important to emphasise in the context of a discussion about the relationship between the proposed Charter of Fundamental Rights and enlargement that it is already the position that a high standard of human rights protection is required of all applicant states. Indeed, Mr Eicke, for Liberty, told the House of Lords Select Committee that he believed that

'[...]what was being expected of those countries constituted a higher level of protection than that required of States in the Union.'[6]

The Commission has also been very thorough in its monitoring of the actual practice in the applicant states and not simply looked at the formal position in their constitutions or assumed that because they have signed the European Convention that everything is necessarily satisfactory. It is recognised that respect for human rights rests ultimately on the development of a deep democratic culture throughout society and must pervade all public and private institutions. The Commission has thus commented critically about issues such as government interference in the media, the treatment of prisoners and conditions in children's institutions in specific countries and more generally on the treatment of minorities. This regular monitoring of the political situation in the applicant states has given the EU considerable leverage and the improvement in the position of the large Russian minorities in Latvia and Estonia is one important example of the influence that has been exerted. A high standard of protection of fundamental rights is therefore already high on the enlargement agenda as a requirement of membership and the proposed Charter is only intended to ensure that a similar high standard is maintained in relation to the institutions and actions of the EU itself. Indeed, it might answer those cynics among the political elite in Central and Eastern Europe that have observed that if the European Union applied to join itself, it ran the risk of not meeting the Copenhagen criteria!

Support for the Charter of Fundamental Rights in the applicant states

Since it was recognised that the Charter would have significant implications for the applicant states, it was agreed that they should be kept fully informed of the work of the Convention responsible for drafting it and given the formal opportunity to present their positions. At a meeting on 19 June 2000 representatives of all thirteen of the current applicants were invited to give their views and those that wished to do so also submitted formal papers which have been made available on the Charter web-site.[7] There was a clear consensus that the Charter is a welcome and positive development that will raise the profile of the EU in the applicant states as a standard bearer of democratic rights and contribute to the strengthening of a democratic culture in the new democracies. The Slovak representative, Daniel Lipsic, referred to their

> '[...] recent tragic experience with the communist totalitarian system and the continuing struggle with the remnants imprinted by the communist ideology in the minds of the people [...]'[8]

and many other delegates also acknowledged the legacy of the communist period. Eugen Dijmarescu, Head of the Romanian Department for European Affairs, expressed the view that

> '[...] while major progress has been made in the area of human rights, particularly in recent years, achieving and securing general respect for human rights continues to remain one of the most important political tasks of the 21ˢᵗ century.'[9]

Any initiative to raise the profile of fundamental rights in the public eye is seen as valuable and the Latvian representative pointed out that the original purpose of the Charter of Fundamental Rights as stated at the Cologne Council was '[...] to make their overriding importance and relevance more visible to the Union's citizens.'

Perhaps precisely because their democratic systems are so new, there seems to be more enthusiasm and interest generally in the whole concept of rights than in many of the existing Member States. All of the representatives from Central and Eastern Europe were particularly keen to emphasise that their states would have no difficulty in adopting the Charter as their own constitutions already contain a very comprehensive list of rights and they have all ratified the ECHR and several other international conventions. Furthermore, whereas the inclusion of social and economic as well as civil and political rights has been a problem in some west European states, in Central and Eastern Europe it was specifically welcomed as being very much in line with their own broad concept of fundamental rights, an important positive legacy of the communist period.

Thus Mr Dijmarescu expressed the opinion that

'[...] the added value brought about by the Charter is that it attempts to incorporate, alongside the basic provisions of the European Convention of Human Rights and the UN Pacts, also the relevant ones from the European Social Charter, placing these distinct categories of rights virtually on the same level of protection.'[10]

The only reservation in some candidate states is if it is decided that the Charter should introduce new justiciable as opposed to aspirational social and economic rights. This is, however, a view shared with several EU Member States. The same is true with respect to the new generation of rights related to recent developments in technology, biology and medicine where the general principles are welcomed but there is some concern that if they are translated into directives they will add to the *acquis* and 'pose new requirements in the context of the accession negotiations.'[11] Overwhelmingly, therefore the response to the draft Charter in the applicant states has been positive but not entirely uncritical and they hope that their views will be taken into consideration before it is finally adopted. Two areas of concern are particularly relevant to the general debate on the Charter: the almost complete absence of reference to minority rights and the danger of competing with rather than complementing the ECHR and undermining the important role of the Court of Human Rights in Strasbourg.

The need to strengthen minority rights

The Hungarian Government has been particularly critical of the almost exclusive concentration on individual rights and the scant reference to the collective rights of minority communities. Although 'membership of a national minority' is one of the grounds on which discrimination is prohibited (Article 21), there is no specific chapter devoted to rights which such groups should be able to enjoy. Even in the sensitive area of education, parents are not given the right to have their children educated in their national language or reflecting their cultural traditions whereas their right to

'[...] ensure the education and teaching in conformity with their religious, philosophical and pedagogical convictions shall be guaranteed' (Article 14).

The neglect of minority rights is particularly surprising as they are expressly recognised in the Copenhagen criteria for EU membership, which go beyond simply specifying non-discrimination and require 'respect for and protection of minorities.' The Commission in its Opinions and Annual Progress Reports has monitored the treatment of national minorities extremely thoroughly and made it quite clear that affirmative action to protect their interests is expected. As has already been mentioned, both Latvia and Estonia have been under pressure to improve the legal and social position of the large Russian minorities in their states. Romania and Slovakia have similarly been encouraged to take positive steps to protect the interests of their Hungarian minorities and the treatment of the Roma throughout Central and Eastern Europe has been criticised by both the Commission and the European Parliament. Furthermore, one of the main reasons Turkey is still excluded from the accession negotiations is its failure to respect and protect the rights of the Kurdish minority.

Not only does the EU therefore seem to be guilty of double standards, with one set of rules for the applicant states and another for its own institutions, but it also seems to be failing to get to grips with what is undoubtedly the greatest potential problem in relation to fundamental rights in Central and Eastern Europe, namely the presence of significant national minority groups in most of the states. As has been seen in the Balkans, this kind of patchwork quilt of national communities is potentially fragile and it is clearly in the interests of the Union to use every possible opportunity to set benchmarks for the proper treatment of minorities. The Hungarian and Slovenian Governments, both particularly concerned about the position of their nationals in neighbouring states, will therefore be pressing for the Charter to be strengthened in relation to minorities.

The danger of two human rights regimes in Europe

The other major concern shared by all the applicant states is the relationship between the EU's Charter of Fundamental Rights and the Council of Europe's Convention on Human Rights (ECHR) which has been in operation for nearly fifty years and has now been ratified by almost every European state. For the first time in European history virtually all people on the continent are living under a common human rights regime and have recourse to the same court for their protection. However, this unique period is in danger of being cut short by the creation of a different, and potentially competing, system of rights under the auspices of the EU. One of the problems is that although the EU's Charter is modelled on the ECHR, it differs quite significantly both in terms of its scope and the actual wording used in otherwise similar articles. The risk of confusion and even conflicts is therefore only too obvious. Furthermore, if the Charter of Fundamental Rights were to be incorporated into the TEU and thereby given legal status, there would be the real risk of conflicting jurisprudence between the European Court of Justice and the European Court of Human Rights in Strasbourg based on different interpretations and, over time, bodies of distinct case-law.

Many other states, non-governmental organisations and institutions such as the European Parliament, the Parliamentary Assembly of the Council of Europe and the House of Lords have expressed similar concerns. Mr Krüger, giving evidence on behalf of the Council of Europe to the House of Lords enquiry, vividly described the potential danger

> '[...] that Europe is divided into two parts, one in the east, one in the west, one for the Council of Europe, one for the European Union, one for the rich, one for the poor.'[12]

However, these fears are felt particularly strongly in Central and Eastern Europe for two specific reasons. Firstly, the Council of Europe is held in much higher regard than is generally the case in Western Europe, where it is largely unknown outside a small political and legal elite. This higher public profile is largely attributable to the fact that it was the first major western organisation to open its doors to the new democracies in the early 1990s. By accrediting their political transformation, the Council of Europe itself acquired enormous status as the moral custodian of democratic values and human rights. There is therefore a genuine desire in the new democracies not to risk weakening either the Council of Europe itself or the Court of Human Rights by exposing it to potential competition from the ECJ. It is also more acutely recognised in Central and Eastern Europe that the Council of Europe's unique contribution is the extent to which it embraces virtually the whole continent. All the CEE applicants except the Czech Republic have neighbours that are unlikely to become EU members for many years, if indeed ever. It is vitally important to them that those non-EU candidate states have ratified the ECHR as democratic stability would be undermined if the authority of the pan-European Strasbourg Court were to be weakened in any way. The solution favoured by most of the applicant states is the one advocated by the Commission and European Parliament, and indeed many other institutions and experts: the EU itself should accede to the ECHR. However, it remains a highly controversial proposal and is unlikely to be agreed at the European Council at Nice.

Conclusion: Will the Charter delay enlargement?

It is because so many issues concerning the scope and legal status of the Charter are controversial that the candidate states fear that it might be the cause of a deferment of the conclusion of the IGC and hence a set-back to the anticipated enlargement timetable. Therefore, they are almost unanimous in calling for its adoption as a purely political declaration of principles at Nice rather than its incorporation into the Treaty at this stage.[13] Their over-riding objective is that the IGC should be concluded on schedule in December 2000 and the revised Treaty ratified in time for the EU to be in a position to honour its commitment to 'be ready' for enlargement by the end of 2002. Already, there is widespread speculation that even a first wave of enlargement is unlikely before 2005. The inclusion of new highly contentious issues on the IGC agenda at this late stage would be seen in the applicant states as yet another ploy by a reluctant Union to delay their accession. Even if the Member States found themselves unexpectedly able to reach a consensus, the ratification of a Treaty containing the Charter of Fundamental Rights by all national parliaments, and in some cases also popular referenda, would be lengthy and problematic. Some applicants also fear that if the Charter is justiciable, it will

> 'create new standards in the *acquis* of the Union, thus going beyond the present standards and posing new requirements in the context of accession negotiations.'[14]

So there is a danger that if some Member States push strongly for a more ambitious goal at Nice, it will be viewed with both suspicion and dismay in at least some of the candidate countries. There is already a strong sense of frustration and disillusionment at the way the timetable for enlargement seems to be constantly slipping. The irony is that in seeking to strengthen human rights in Europe, the very opposite could be the consequence if the hopes of the citizens in the new democracies for EU membership are once more disappointed.

Notes

1 The ten are Bulgaria, the Czech Republic, Estonia, Hungary, Latvia, Lithuania, Romania, Slovakia, Slovenia and Poland.

[2] See House of Lords Select Committee on the European Communities. 'The EU Charter of Fundamental Rights'. Session 1999-2000, 8th Report.

3 '*Acquis*' is the term used to cover the whole range of principles, policies, laws, practices, obligations and objectives that have been agreed within the European Union.

4 Article F(2) TEU.

[5] Presidency Conclusions, Copenhagen European Council, June 1993.

[6] House of Lords Select Committee, op. cit. paragraph 114.

[7] See www.consilium.eu.int. Those states such as Hungary that did not submit a formal paper apparently decided that in view of the divergence of views between the Member States it would be strategically better not to appear to be taking sides.

8 CHARTE 4395/00, available on the Charter web site at www.consilium.eu.int

[9] CHARTE 4377/00, ibid.

[10] Ibid.

[11] CHARTE 4376/00, ibid.

[12] House of Lords Select Committee, op. cit., paragraph 96.

[13] *Agence Europe,* 21 June 2000.

[14] This was the view of the Mrs Antoinette Primatarova, the Bulgarian Ambassador to the EU. See CHARTE 4376/00.

Annex I

DRAFT CHARTER OF FUNDAMENTAL RIGHTS OF THE EUROPEAN UNION

Brussels, 28 September 2000
CHARTE 4487/00
CONVENT 50

PREAMBLE

The peoples of Europe, in creating an ever closer union among them, are resolved to share a peaceful future based on common values.

Conscious of its spiritual and moral heritage, the Union is founded on the indivisible, universal values of human dignity, freedom, equality and solidarity; it is based on the principles of democracy and the rule of law. It places the individual at the heart of its activities, by establishing the citizenship of the Union and by creating an area of freedom, security and justice.

The Union contributes to the preservation and to the development of these common values while respecting the diversity of the cultures and traditions of the peoples of Europe as well as the national identities of the Member States and the organisation of their public authorities at national, regional and local levels; it seeks to promote balanced and sustainable development and ensures free movement of persons, goods, services and capital, and the freedom of establishment.

To this end, it is necessary to strengthen the protection of fundamental rights in the light of changes in society, social progress and scientific and technological developments by making those rights more visible in a Charter.

This Charter reaffirms, with due regard for the powers and tasks of the Community and the Union and the principle of subsidiarity, the rights as they result, in particular, from the constitutional traditions and international obligations common to the Member States, the Treaty on European Union, the Community Treaties, the European Convention for the Protection of Human Rights and Fundamental Freedoms, the Social Charters adopted by the Community and by the Council of Europe and the case law of the Court of Justice of the European Communities and of the European Court of Human Rights.

Enjoyment of these rights entails responsibilities and duties with regard to other persons, to the human community and to future generations.

The Union therefore recognises the rights, freedoms and principles set out hereafter.

CHAPTER I
DIGNITY

Article 1

Human dignity

Human dignity is inviolable. It must be respected and protected.

Article 2

Right to life

1. Everyone has the right to life.

2. No one shall be condemned to the death penalty, or executed.

Article 3

Right to the integrity of the person

1. Everyone has the right to respect for his or her physical and mental integrity.

2. In the fields of medicine and biology, the following must be respected in particular:

- the free and informed consent of the person concerned, according to the procedures laid down by law,

- the prohibition of eugenic practices, in particular those aiming at the selection of persons,

- the prohibition on making the human body and its parts as such a source of financial gain,

- the prohibition of the reproductive cloning of human beings.

Article 4

Prohibition of torture and inhuman or degrading treatment or punishment

No one shall be subjected to torture or to inhuman or degrading treatment or punishment.

Article 5

Prohibition of slavery and forced labour

1. No one shall be held in slavery or servitude.

2. No one shall be required to perform forced or compulsory labour.

3. Trafficking in human beings is prohibited.

CHAPTER II
FREEDOMS

Article 6

Right to liberty and security
Everyone has the right to liberty and security of person.

Article 7

Respect for private and family life
Everyone has the right to respect for his or her private and family life, home and communications.

Article 8

Protection of personal data

1. Everyone has the right to the protection of personal data concerning him or her.

2. Such data must be processed fairly for specified purposes and on the basis of the consent of the person concerned or some other legitimate basis laid down by law. Everyone has the right of access to data which has been collected concerning him or her, and the right to have it rectified.

3. Compliance with these rules shall be subject to control by an independent authority.

Article 9

Right to marry and right to found a family

The right to marry and the right to found a family shall be guaranteed in accordance with the national laws governing the exercise of these rights.

Article 10

Freedom of thought, conscience and religion

1. Everyone has the right to freedom of thought, conscience and religion. This right includes freedom to change religion or belief and freedom, either alone or in community with others and in public or in private, to manifest religion or belief, in worship, teaching, practice and observance.

2. The right to conscientious objection is recognised, in accordance with the national laws governing the exercise of this right.

Article 11

Freedom of expression and information

1. Everyone has the right to freedom of expression. This right shall include freedom to hold opinions and to receive and

impart information and ideas without interference by public authority and regardless of frontiers.

2. The freedom and pluralism of the media shall be respected.

Article 12

Freedom of assembly and of association

1. Everyone has the right to freedom of peaceful assembly and to freedom of association at all levels, in particular in political, trade union and civic matters, which implies the right of everyone to form and to join trade unions for the protection of his or her interests.

2. Political parties at Union level contribute to expressing the political will of the citizens of the Union.

Article 13

Freedom of the arts and sciences

The arts and scientific research shall be free of constraint. Academic freedom shall be respected.

Article 14

Right to education

1. Everyone has the right to education and to have access to vocational and continuing training.

2. This right includes the possibility to receive free compulsory education.

3. The freedom to found educational establishments with due respect for democratic principles and the right of parents to ensure the education and teaching of their children in conformity with their religious, philosophical and pedagogical convictions shall be respected, in accordance with the national laws governing the exercise of such freedom and right.

Article 15

Freedom to choose an occupation and right to engage in work

1. Everyone has the right to engage in work and to pursue a freely chosen or accepted occupation.

2. Every citizen of the Union has the freedom to seek employment, to work, to exercise the right of establishment and to provide services in any Member State.

3. Nationals of third countries who are authorised to work in the territories of the Member States are entitled to working conditions equivalent to those of citizens of the Union.

Article 16

Freedom to conduct a business

The freedom to conduct a business in accordance with Community law and national laws and practices is recognised.

Article 17

Right to property

1. Everyone has the right to own, use, dispose of and bequeath his or her lawfully acquired possessions. No one may be deprived of his or her possessions, except in the public interest and in the cases and under the conditions provided for by law, subject to fair compensation being paid in good time for their loss. The use of property may be regulated by law insofar as is necessary for the general interest.

2. Intellectual property shall be protected.

Article 18

Right to asylum

The right to asylum shall be guaranteed with due respect for the rules of the Geneva Convention of 28 July 1951 and the Protocol of 31 January 1967 relating to the status of refugees and in accordance with the Treaty establishing the European Community.

Article 19

Protection in the event of removal, expulsion or extradition

1. Collective expulsions are prohibited.

2. No one may be removed, expelled or extradited to a State where there is a serious risk that he or she would be subjected to the death penalty, torture or other inhuman or degrading treatment or punishment.

CHAPTER III
EQUALITY

Article 20

Equality before the law

Everyone is equal before the law.

Article 21

Non-discrimination

1. Any discrimination based on any ground such as sex, race, colour, ethnic or social origin, genetic features, language, religion or belief, political or any other opinion, membership of a national minority, property, birth, disability, age or sexual orientation shall be prohibited.

2. Within the scope of application of the Treaty establishing the European Community and of the Treaty on European Union, and without prejudice to the special provisions of those Treaties, any discrimination on grounds of nationality shall be prohibited.

Article 22

Cultural, religious and linguistic diversity

The Union shall respect cultural, religious and linguistic diversity.

Article 23

Equality between men and women

Equality between men and women must be ensured in all areas, including employment, work and pay.

The principle of equality shall not prevent the maintenance or adoption of measures providing for specific advantages in favour of the under-represented sex.

Article 24

The rights of the child

1. Children shall have the right to such protection and care as is necessary for their well-being.

They may express their views freely. Such views shall be taken into consideration on matters which concern them in accordance with their age and maturity.

2. In all actions relating to children, whether taken by public authorities or private institutions, the child's best interests must be a primary consideration.

3. Every child shall have the right to maintain on a regular basis a personal relationship and direct contact with both his or her parents, unless that is contrary to his or her interests.

Article 25

The rights of the elderly

The Union recognises and respects the rights of the elderly to lead a life of dignity and independence and to participate in social and cultural life.

Article 26

Integration of persons with disabilities

The Union recognises and respects the right of persons with disabilities to benefit from measures designed to ensure their independence, social and occupational integration and participation in the life of the community.

CHAPTER IV
SOLIDARITY
Article 27

Workers' right to information and consultation within the undertaking

Workers or their representatives must, at the appropriate levels, be guaranteed information and consultation in good time in the cases and under the conditions provided for by Community law and national laws and practices.

Article 28

Right of collective bargaining and action

Workers and employers, or their respective organisations, have, in accordance with Community law and national laws and practices, the right to negotiate and conclude collective agreements at the appropriate levels and, in cases of conflicts of interest, to take collective action to defend their interests, including strike action.

Article 29

Right of access to placement services

Everyone has the right of access to a free placement service.

Article 30

Protection in the event of unjustified dismissal

Every worker has the right to protection against unjustified dismissal, in accordance with Community law and national laws and practices.

Article 31

Fair and just working conditions

1. Every worker has the right to working conditions which respect his or her health, safety and dignity.

2. Every worker has the right to limitation of maximum working hours, to daily and weekly rest periods and to an annual period of paid leave.

Article 32

Prohibition of child labour and protection of young people at work

The employment of children is prohibited. The minimum age of admission to employment may not be lower than the minimum school-leaving age, without prejudice to such rules as may be more favourable to young people and except for limited derogations.

Young people admitted to work must have working conditions appropriate to their age and be protected against economic exploitation and any work likely to harm their safety, health or physical, mental, moral or social development or to interfere with their education.

Article 33

Family and professional life

1. The family shall enjoy legal, economic and social protection.

2. To reconcile family and professional life, everyone shall have the right to protection from dismissal for a reason connected with maternity and the right to paid maternity leave and to parental leave following the birth or adoption of a child.

Article 34

Social security and social assistance

1. The Union recognises and respects the entitlement to social security benefits and social services providing protection in cases such as maternity, illness, industrial accidents, dependency or old age, and in the case of loss of employment, in accordance with the procedures laid down by Community law and national laws and practices.

2. Everyone residing and moving legally within the European

Union is entitled to social security benefits and social advantages in accordance with Community law and national laws and practices.

3. In order to combat social exclusion and poverty, the Union recognises and respects the right to social and housing assistance so as to ensure a decent existence for all those who lack sufficient resources, in accordance with the procedures laid down by Community law and national laws and practices.

Article 35

Health care

Everyone has the right of access to preventive health care and the right to benefit from medical treatment under the conditions established by national laws and practices. A high level of human health protection shall be ensured in the definition and implementation of all Union policies and activities.

Article 36

Access to services of general economic interest

The Union recognises and respects access to services of general economic interest as provided for in national laws and practices, in accordance with the Treaty establishing the European Community, in order to promote the social and territorial cohesion of the Union.

Article 37

Environmental protection

A high level of environmental protection and the improvement of the quality of the environment must be integrated into the polices of the Union and ensured in accordance with the principle of sustainable development.

Article 38

Consumer Protection

Union policies shall ensure a high level of consumer protection.

CHAPTER V
CITIZENS' RIGHTS
Article 39

Right to vote and to stand as a candidate at elections to the European Parliament

1. Every citizen of the Union has the right to vote and to stand as a candidate at elections to the European Parliament in the Member State in which he or she resides, under the same conditions as nationals of that State.

2. Members of the European Parliament shall be elected by direct universal suffrage in a free and secret ballot.

Article 40

Right to vote and to stand as a candidate at municipal elections

Every citizen of the Union has the right to vote and to stand as a candidate at municipal elections in the Member State in which he or she resides under the same conditions as nationals of that State.

Article 41

Right to good administration

1. Every person has the right to have his or her affairs handled impartially, fairly and within a reasonable time by the institutions and bodies of the Union.

2. This right includes:

- the right of every person to be heard, before any individual measure which would affect him or her adversely is taken;

- the right of every person to have access to his or her file, while respecting the legitimate interests of confidentiality and of professional and business secrecy;

- the obligation of the administration to give reasons for its decisions.

3. Every person has the right to have the Community make good any damage caused by its institutions or by its servants in the performance of their duties, in accordance with the general principles common to the laws of the Member States.

4. Every person may write to the institutions of the Union in one of the languages of the Treaties and must have an answer in the same language.

Article 42

Right of access to documents

Any citizen of the Union, and any natural or legal person residing or having its registered office in a Member State, has a right of access to European Parliament, Council and Commission documents.

Article 43

Ombudsman

Any citizen of the Union and any natural or legal person residing or having its registered office in a Member State has the right to refer to the Ombudsman of the Union cases of maladministration in the activities of the Community institutions or bodies, with the exception of the Court of Justice and the Court of First Instance acting in their judicial role.

Article 44

Right to petition

Any citizen of the Union and any natural or legal person residing or having its registered office in a Member State has the right to petition the European Parliament.

Article 45

Freedom of movement and of residence

1. Every citizen of the Union has the right to move and reside freely within the territory of the Member States.

2. Freedom of movement and residence may be granted, in accordance with the Treaty establishing the European Community, to nationals of third countries legally resident in the territory of a Member State.

Article 46

Diplomatic and consular protection

Every citizen of the Union shall, in the territory of a third country in which the Member State of which he or she is a national is not represented, be entitled to protection by the diplomatic or consular authorities of any Member State, on the same conditions as the nationals of that Member State.

CHAPTER VI

JUSTICE

Article 47

Right to an effective remedy and to a fair trial

Everyone whose rights and freedoms guaranteed by the law of the Union are violated has the right to an effective remedy before a tribunal in compliance with the conditions laid down in this Article.

Everyone is entitled to a fair and public hearing within a reasonable time by an independent and impartial tribunal previously established by law. Everyone shall have the possibility of being advised, defended and represented.

Legal aid shall be made available to those who lack sufficient resources insofar as such aid is necessary to ensure effective access to justice.

Article 48

Presumption of innocence and right of defence

1. Everyone who has been charged shall be presumed innocent until proved guilty according to law.

2. Respect for the rights of the defence of anyone who has been charged shall be guaranteed.

Article 49

Principles of legality and proportionality of criminal offences and penalties

1. No one shall be held guilty of any criminal offence on account of any act or omission which did not constitute a criminal offence under national law or international law at the time when it was committed. Nor shall a heavier penalty be imposed than that which was applicable at the time the criminal offence was committed. If, subsequent to the commission of a criminal offence, the law provides for a lighter penalty, that penalty shall be applicable.

2. This Article shall not prejudice the trial and punishment of any person for any act or omission which, at the time when it was committed, was criminal according to the general principles recognised by the community of nations.

3. The severity of penalties must not be disproportionate to the criminal offence.

Article 50

Right not to be tried or punished twice in criminal proceedings for the same criminal offence

No one shall be liable to be tried or punished again in criminal proceedings for an offence for which he or she has already been finally acquitted or convicted within the Union in accordance with the law.

CHAPTER VII

GENERAL PROVISIONS

Article 51

Scope

1. The provisions of this Charter are addressed to the institutions and bodies of the Union with due regard for the principle of subsidiarity and to the Member States only when they are implementing Union law. They shall therefore respect the rights, observe the principles and promote the application thereof in accordance with their respective powers.

2. This Charter does not establish any new power or task for the Community or the Union, or modify powers and tasks defined by the Treaties.

Article 52

Scope of guaranteed rights

1. Any limitation on the exercise of the rights and freedoms recognised by this Charter must be provided for by law and respect the essence of those rights and freedoms. Subject to the principle of proportionality, limitations may be made only if they are necessary and genuinely meet objectives of general interest recognized by the Union or the need to protect the rights and freedoms of others.

2. Rights recognised by this Charter which are based on the Community Treaties or the Treaty on European Union shall be exercised under the conditions and within the limits defined by those Treaties.

3. Insofar as this Charter contains rights which correspond to rights guaranteed by the Convention for the Protection of Human Rights and Fundamental Freedoms, the meaning and scope of those rights shall be the same as those laid down by the said Convention. This provision shall not prevent Union law providing more extensive protection.

Article 53

Level of protection

Nothing in this Charter shall be interpreted as restricting or adversely affecting human rights and fundamental freedoms as recognised, in their respective fields of application, by Union law and international law and by international agreements to which the Union, the Community or all the Member States are party, including the European Convention for the Protection of Human Rights and Fundamental Freedoms, and by the Member States' constitutions.

Article 54

Prohibition of abuse of rights

Nothing in this Charter shall be interpreted as implying any right to engage in any activity or to perform any act aimed at the destruction of any of the rights and freedoms recognised in this Charter or at their limitation to a greater extent than is provided for herein.

Annex II

European Council Conclusions

This annex contains the relevant passages on the EU Charter from the European Council Conclusions of the Summit meetings in Cologne in June 1999 and Tampere in October 1999 as well as extracts from the report of the informal meeting of EU Heads of State and Government in Biarritz in October 2000.

Cologne

'EU Charter of Fundamental Rights

44. The European Council takes the view that, at the present stage of development of the European Union, the fundamental rights applicable at Union level should be consolidated in a Charter and thereby made more evident.

45. To this end it has adopted the Decision appended as Annex IV. The incoming Presidency is asked to establish the conditions for the implementation of this Decision by the time of the extraordinary meeting of the European Council in Tampere on 15 and 16 October 1999.'

ANNEX IV

EUROPEAN COUNCIL DECISION ON THE DRAWING UP OF A CHARTER OF FUNDAMENTAL RIGHTS OF THE EUROPEAN UNION

Protection of fundamental rights is a founding principle of the Union and an indispensable prerequisite for her legitimacy. The obligation of the Union to respect fundamental rights has been confirmed and defined by the jurisprudence of the European Court of Justice. There appears to be a need, at the present stage of the Union's development, to establish a Charter of fundamental rights in order to make their overriding importance and relevance more visible to the Union's citizens.

The European Council believes that this Charter should contain the fundamental rights and freedoms as well as basic procedural rights guaranteed by the European Convention for the Protection of Human Rights and Fundamental Freedoms and derived from the constitutional traditions common to the Member States, as general principles of Community law. The Charter should also include the fundamental rights that pertain only to the Union's citizens. In drawing up such a Charter account should furthermore be taken of economic and social rights as contained in the European Social Charter and the Community Charter of the Fundamental Social Rights of Workers (Article 136 TEC), insofar as they do not merely establish objectives for action by the Union.

In the view of the European Council, a draft of such a Charter of Fundamental Rights of the European Union should be elaborated by a body composed of representatives of the Heads of State and Government and of the President of the Commission as well as of members of the European Parliament and national parliaments. Representatives of the European Court of Justice should participate as observers. Representatives of the Economic and Social Committee, the Committee of the Regions and social groups as well as experts should be invited to give their views. Secretariat services should be provided by the General Secretariat of the Council.

This body should present a draft document in advance of the European Council in December 2000. The European Council will propose to the European Parliament and the Commission that, together with the Council, they should solemnly proclaim on the basis of the draft document a European Charter of Fundamental Rights. It will then have to be considered whether and, if so, how the Charter should be integrated into the treaties. The European Council mandates the General Affairs Council to take the necessary steps prior to the Tampere European Council.

Tampere

'In close connection with the area of freedom, security and justice, the European Council has agreed on the composition, method of work and practical arrangements (attached in the annex) for the body entrusted with drawing up a draft Charter of fundamental rights of the European Union. It invites all parties involved to ensure that work on the Charter can begin rapidly.'

ANNEX

COMPOSITION METHOD OF WORK AND PRACTICAL ARRANGEMENTS FOR THE BODY TO ELABORATE A DRAFT EU CHARTER OF FUNDAMENTAL RIGHTS, AS SET OUT IN THE COLOGNE CONCLUSIONS

A. COMPOSITION OF THE BODY

(i) Members

(a) Heads of State or Government of Member States
Fifteen representatives of the Heads of State or Government of Member States.

(b) Commission
One representative of the President of the European Commission.

(c) European Parliament
Sixteen members of the European Parliament to be designated by itself.

(d) National Parliaments
Thirty members of national Parliaments (two from each national Parliament) to be designated by national Parliaments themselves.

Members of the Body may be replaced by alternates in the event of being unable to attend meetings of the Body.

(ii) Chairperson and Vice-Chairpersons of the Body
The Chairperson of the Body shall be elected by the Body. A member of the European Parliament, a member of a national Parliament, and the representative of the President of the

European Council if not elected to the Chair, shall act as Vice-Chairpersons of the Body.

The member of the European Parliament acting as Vice-Chairperson shall be elected by the members of the European Parliament serving on the Body. The member of a national Parliament acting as Vice-Chairperson shall be elected by the members of national Parliaments serving on the Body.

(iii) Observers

Two representatives of the Court of Justice of the European Communities to be designated by the Court.

Two representatives of the Council of Europe, including one from the European Court of Human Rights.

(iv) Bodies of the European Union to be invited to give their views

The Economic and Social Committee

The Committee of the Regions

The Ombudsman

(v) Exchange of views with the applicant States

An appropriate exchange of views should be held by the Body or by the Chairperson with the applicant States.

(vi) Other bodies, social groups or experts to be invited to give their views

Other bodies, social groups and experts may be invited by the Body to give their views.

(vii) Secretariat

The General Secretariat of the Council shall provide the Body with secretariat services. To ensure proper coordination, close contacts will be established with the General Secretariat of the European Parliament, with the Commission and, to the extent necessary, with the secretariats of the national Parliaments.

B. WORKING METHODS OF THE BODY

(i) Preparation

The Chairperson of the Body shall, in close concertation with the Vice-Chairpersons, propose a work plan for the Body and perform other appropriate preparatory work.

(ii) Transparency of the proceedings

In principle, hearings held by the Body and documents submitted at such hearings should be public.

(iii) Working groups

The Body may establish *ad hoc* working groups, which shall be open to all members of the Body.

(iv) Drafting

On the basis of the work plan agreed by the Body, a Drafting Committee composed of the Chairperson, the Vice-Chairpersons and the representative of the Commission and assisted by the General Secretariat of the Council, shall elaborate a preliminary Draft Charter, taking account of drafting proposals submitted by any member of the Body.

Each of the three Vice-Chairpersons shall regularly consult with the respective component part of the Body from which he or she emanates.

(v) Elaboration of the Draft Charter by the Body

When the Chairperson, in close concertation with the Vice-Chairpersons, deems that the text of the draft Charter elaborated by the Body can eventually be subscribed to by all the parties, it shall be forwarded to the European Council through the normal preparatory procedure.

C. PRACTICAL ARRANGEMENTS

The Body shall hold its meetings in Brussels, alternately in the Council and the European Parliament buildings.

A complete language regime shall be applicable for sessions of the Body.

Biarritz

'II. The European Union's Charter of Fundamental Rights

After having listened to a report by G. Braibant, in the name of President Herzog, absent for health reasons, the European Council approved the content of the charter of fundamental rights and congratulated itself on the contribution this text brings to the model for values and society that the European union constitutes.

Once formally adopted by the European Commission and the European Parliament, this text will be solemly announced by the European Council of Nice.'

Annex III

The Council of Europe and the European Convention for the Protection of Human Rights and Fundamental Freedoms

Some key dates in the history of the Council of Europe

5 May 1949	Belgium, Denmark, France, Ireland, Italy, Luxembourg, the Netherlands, Norway, Sweden and the UK sign the **Treaty of London** which establishes the **Council of Europe**
4 Nov 1950	The **Convention for the Protection of Human Rights and Fundamental Freedoms (ECHR)** is signed in Rome as the first legal instrument safeguarding human rights (in force in 1953)
18 Sept 1959	The Council establishes the **European Court of Human Rights** in Strasbourg to ensure the observance of the obligations undertaken by the contracting states (in force in 1953)
18 Oct 1961	The **European Social Charter** is signed in Turin as the Council's economic and social counterpart of the ECHR (in force in 1965, revised in 1996)
15 Oct 1985	The **European Charter of Local Self-Government** is signed
26 Nov 1987	The **European Convention for the Prevention of Torture and Inhuman or Degrading Treatment or Punishment** is signed
8/9 Oct 1993	First **Council of Europe Summit of Heads of State and Government in Vienna** adopts a declaration confirming its pan-European vocation and setting new political priorities in protection national minorities and combating all forms of racism, xenophobia and intolerance
1 Feb 1995	The **Framework Convention of the Protection of National Minorities** is signed

4 April 1997	The Council sings the **European Convention on Human Rights and Biomedicine**
10/11 Oct 1997	Second **Summit of Heads of State and Government in Strasbourg**
12 Jan 1998	An **Additional Protocol to the European Convention on Human Rights and Biomedicine** is signed, prohibiting the cloning of human beings
1 Nov 1998	A single permanent European Court of Human Rights is established in Strasbourg under **Protocol 11** to the ECHR, replacing the existing system
5 May 1999	The Council of Europe celebrates its **50th anniversary**

Some facts about the Council of Europe and the ECHR

The Council of Europe aims to protect human rights, pluralist democracy and the rule of law, to promote awareness and encourage the development of Europe's cultural identity and diversity, to seek solutions to problems facing European society (discrimination against minorities, xenophobia, intolerance, environmental protection, human cloning, Aids, drugs, organised crime, etc.) and to help consolidate democratic stability in Europe by backing political, legislative and constitutional reform.

Membership of this intergovernmental organisation is open to any European state provided it accepts the principle of the rule of law and guarantees human rights and fundamental freedoms to everyone under its jurisdiction. The Council of Europe currently has 41 members, thereby covering the whole of Europe. Most recent members include Russia and other former Soviet states whose understanding of fundamental rights has been a different one from that in the West. The improvement of human rights protection is one of the many challenges these countries face in their transition to democracy and rule of law.

The Council's work leads to European conventions and agreements which are a basis for the harmonisation and amendment of national legislation of the member states as well as non-members. A form of variable geometry allows for co-operation between some states to carry out a specific activity of common interest, by Partial Agreements, if the other member states need to give their consent.

The Council of Europe operates through the following bodies: Committee of Ministers, Parliamentary Assembly, Congress of Local and Regional Authorities of Europe and permanent Secretariat .

Freedom and fundamental rights

The Council of Europe works towards the better protection of human rights in four main areas: Effective supervision and protection of fundamental freedoms; identifying new threats to human rights and human dignity; developing public awareness of the importance of human rights; and promoting human rights education and professional training.

European Convention on Human Rights (ECHR)

The most significant instrument is the ECHR which sets out the inalienable civil and political rights and freedoms of each individual. As an international treaty it is directed at its signatory states which are, by virtue of Article 1 ECHR, obliged to guarantee these rights to everyone within their jurisdiction - regardless of their nationality. The ECHR was inspired by the United Nations Universal Declaration of Human Rights of 1948 and presented a first step in realising the collective enforcement of certain rights stated therein.

Rights enshrined in the ECHR include the right to life, protection against inhuman treatment, freedom and safety, a fair trial and an effective remedy, marry and respect for one's private and family life, one's home and one's correspondence, peaceful enjoyment of possessions, education and free elections. Freedom from discrimination, freedom of expression, thought, conscience and religion and freedom of peaceful assembly and association are guaranteed; torture, slavery and forced labour are prohibited. These rights are not entirely unqualified, and states retain some discretion to adopt derogations, in certain circumstances.

International enforcement mechanisms ensure that fundamental rights are observed. Whereas alleged violations by contracting states originally had to be examined as to their admissibility in a lengthy procedure by the European Commission of Human Rights before claims could be brought before the Court, complaints can now be referred directly to the European Court of Human Rights (ECtHR) in Strasbourg by states, and by individuals where parties have recognised a right of individual petition. The judgements of the Court are binding on the states concerned which have to ensure compliance, i.e. compensate the applicant and avoid any similar violations in future. To ensure enforcement, the Committee of Ministers has the power to suspend or, as a last resort, expel a non-compliant member.

The ECtHR's case-law has further developed fundamental rights and constant review of the ECHR has resulted in 11 Protocols to the Convention extending and enhancing the protection afforded to individuals.

In the UK, the Human Rights Act 1998 has incorporated the Convention into domestic law in October 2000. This means that individuals can now bring actions against violations of their rights protected in the ECHR in proceedings before UK courts. However, the UK has not signed up to Protocol 4, which concerns contractual obligations, free movement rights and expulsions of nationals and aliens, and has not yet ratified Protocol 7 which also adds to the protection of immigrants and refugees, to procedural and substantial rights in respect of judicial proceedings and to equality between spouses.

A new Protocol (No 12) has been adopted by the Committee of Ministers and will be open for signature by member states from 4 November 2000. Protocol 12 provides a general prohibition of discrimination, removing the limitations on the non-discrimination provision in Article 14 ECHR. It is as yet unclear whether the UK will sign up to this Protocol.

European Social Charter

The European Social Charter and the Additional Protocols guarantee a series of fundamental rights concerning conditions of employment (e.g. non-discrimination and equal pay, prohibition of forced labour, trade union rights, collective bargaining and right to strike) and social cohesion (e.g. protection of health, social security and social assistance, right to decent housing, health, education and vocational training). The Charter was revised in 1996, adding to the protection afforded in the original treaty. The UK has signed, but not yet ratified the revised Social Charter.

Implementation and conformity to the Charter are monitored by an international system of supervision. Member states must submit reports on its application. These are assessed by the European Committee of Social Rights (ECSR) composed of independent experts. The Committee of Ministers issues recommendations to governments whose national legislation and practice is considered to be in breach of the rights guaranteed in the Charter.

Workers' and employers' organisations and NGOs now also have a right to lodge collective complaints with the ECSR to assess alleged violations of the social rights protected by the treaty. This right does not, however, extend to individuals and the ECtHR has no jurisdiction over the Charter - except for those rights that have also been included into the ECHR.

Some other international treaties established within the Council of Europe framework, such as the European Code of Social Security (1964), the European Convention on Social Security (1972) and the European Convention on the Legal Status of Migrant Workers (1977) provide further protection, equal treatment and non-discrimination rights irrespective of nationality. The UK has so far only ratified the first of these, the Code of Social Security.